Here are six views of Japanese music that are seldom available to Western readers because they are basic to the art and thus little discussed. William Malm begins in the important world of Japanese drum making and looks at the teaching of drum music from a spiritual as well as a pedagogical point of view. After an interlude of general information about Japanese music, he presents four comparative views of specific compositions. The noh and kabuki versions of *Shakkyo* are examples of one story in two genres; *Kanda matsuri* contains two genres (folk festival and concert shamisen music) in one piece. *Horai* is viewed from the perspective of four different performances. The final comparison places one story in two different musical worlds, the noh play *Sumidagawa* and Benjamin Britten's *Curlew River.*

Text translations, drawings, photographs, and a glossary/index enhance the reader's introduction to this rich music tradition, and the music examples are available separately on cassette.

SIX HIDDEN VIEWS OF JAPANESE MUSIC

The Ernest Bloch Professorship of Music and the Ernest Bloch Lectures were established at the University of California in 1962 in order to bring distinguished figures in music to the Berkeley campus from time to time. Made possible by the Jacob and Rosa Stern Musical Fund, the professorship was founded in memory of Ernest Bloch (1880–1959), Professor of Music at Berkeley from 1940 to 1959.

THE ERNEST BLOCH PROFESSORS

1964	Ralph Kirkpatrick
1965–66	Winton Dean
1966–67	Roger Sessions
1968–69	Gerald Abraham
1971	Leonard B. Meyer
1972	Edward T. Cone
1975–76	Donald Jay Grout
1976–77	Charles Rosen
1977–78	Alan Tyson
1979–80	William P. Malm
1980–81	Andrew Porter

William P. Malm

SIX HIDDEN VIEWS
OF JAPANESE MUSIC

90-1941

University of California Press
BERKELEY · LOS ANGELES · LONDON

University of California Press
Berkeley and Los Angeles, California

University of California Press, Ltd.
London, England

© 1986 by
The Regents of the University of California

Library of Congress Cataloging in Publication Data

Malm, William P.
  Six hidden views of Japanese music.

  Includes bibliographical references and index.
    1. Music—Japan—History and
criticism.   I. Title.
II. Title: 6 hidden views of Japanese music.
III. Title: Hidden views of Japanese music.
ML340.M34   1984   781.752   83-17984
ISBN 0-520-05045-2

Printed in the United States of America

     2   3   4   5   6   7   8   9

Available separately from the University of California
Press: William P. Malm, *Six Hidden Views of Japanese
Music*, Cassette of Music Examples. See the list of 54
cassette examples at the beginning of the book.
One hour, two sides, $8.95
ISBN 0-520-05727-9

To TANAKA DENZAEMON XI
A master of the hidden views

CONTENTS

LIST OF FIGURES

LIST OF MUSICAL EXAMPLES

LIST OF
CASSETTE
EXAMPLES

.

The cassette contains excerpts from selected examples transcribed or discussed in the text. Each example is announced by the letter identifying its order on the tape and by its title or, if it is transcribed, the example number in the book. These excerpts are made possible through the kind permission of the recording companies cited in this list and in the footnotes of the text. Complete citations are found at the end of this list. In Examples AA–HH, I = Columbia CL-18, II = Columbia CLS 5060, III = Crown LA 4054, and IV = Victor SJL 2220. Examples II–PP are from a videotape purchased from the Japanese National Broadcasting Corporation and used with their permission.

Cassette letter	Example number or title	Source
A	Example 3	3a, King KHA 19; 3b, Chikuma VP 3022; 3c, Columbia CLS 5099
B	Example 4	4a, King KHA 19; 4b, Chikuma VP 3022
C	Example 5	Chikuma VP 3022
D	Example 6	Chikuma VP 3022
E	Example 7	Chikuma VP 3022
F	A noh excerpt and Example 8a	noh, King KHA 19; 8a, Chikuma VP 3022
G	Example 9	Chikuma VP 3022
H-I	Two nagauta versions of raijo and ranjo (parts shown in Example 12)	Chikuma VP 3022 Columbia CLS 5099
J	A noh version of raijo and ranjo (parts shown in Example 12)	King KHA 19

HH	Example 34	I
II	Example 36	NHK videotape
JJ	Example 42	NHK videotape
KK	Example 45	NHK videotape
LL	Example 48	NHK videotape
MM	Example 50	NHK videotape
NN	Example 52	NHK videotape
OO	Example 54	NHK videotape
PP	The final chorus of *Sumidagawa*	NHK videotape

SUMMARY OF SOURCES BY COMPANY

Japanese records are often short-lived. The materials of this 1981 study were checked against February 1984 holdings of the Bunkado Record Store (Ginza 5-chome 14-1, Chuo-ku, Tokyo). Only the three items marked below with asterisks were still available. Possible substitutes for out-of-print records are listed in parentheses. The original recordings of this study are available at the University of Michigan Music Library.

Chikuma shobō:	*Shakkyō*, VP 3022 in volume 9 of *Hōgaku taikei*
Columbia:	*Hōrai*, CL 18 (now CLS 20; also available are CL 102 and WZ 7005); *Hōrai*, CL 5060*; *Shakkyō*, CL 5099 *Shamisen uta no oitachi to sono utsurikawari* AL 5021
Crown:	*Hōrai*, LA 4054
King:	*Shakkyō*, KHA 19; *Renjishi*, KC 1036 (use Columbia CLS 5005 or CL 41)
Toshiba:	*Kanda matsuri*, JHO 1010 (now THO 6009); *Kanda bayashi*, JPO 1035 (use King KHA 106)
Victor:	*Edo no kagura to matsuri bayashi*, SJ 3004; *Hōrai*, SJL 2220*; *Kanze ryū mai no hayashi*, SJL 111–115 (Hōshō school version is SJL 180–183); *Nihon buyō ongaku*, SJ 3013 (from a set of three volumes); *Shin-Shakkyō*, SLR 557

ACKNOWLEDGMENTS

Among the many colleagues who helped make this study possible, I want especially to thank Professor Bonnie Wade and Professor Ann Pescatello, whose encouragement and hospitality made my experience at the University of California, Berkeley, so rewarding. My Berkeley office neighbor, Professor Daniel Heartz, and other members of the music faculty of the University of California deserve recognition for their tolerance of all the Japanese sounds that emanated from my nonsoundproof office for six straight months, and the department office staff are thanked for their help and efficiency. The Japan Center of the University of California generously provided me with a skilled translation assistant, John R. Mayer, from January to June of 1980, and the Center for Japanese Studies of the University of Michigan gave valuable secretarial and research support during the summers of 1980 and 1981. I am grateful to the Japanese record companies cited in the List of Cassette Examples for permission to duplicate excerpts from their recordings so that the reader can have some sonic frame of reference for the study. Professor Robert Brower and Professor James Crump of the University of Michigan and Professor Thomas Hare of Stanford University provided professional advice on Far Eastern language and literature matters, and the staff of the Japanese music division of the Ueno Music Academy in Tokyo were particularly helpful during the final drafting of the manuscript. Finally, I must thank the many professional Japanese musicians who freely gave of their time and their hidden knowledge in either formal or backstage conversations.

NOTES ON
THE TEXT

In the text of this book Japanese names are given with the family name first. Capitals are not used in the romanization of Japanese words except in the names of schools or guilds and in the first word of a title of a book or composition. Japanese words are italicized only when first used or when defined. Words common in English dictionaries, such as *shamisen* or *koto*, are not italicized, and the French spelling *noh* is used for the Japanese term *nō*. The romanizations of complete song texts in the Third, Fourth, and Fifth Views conform to the Japanese system of using no punctuation and of capitalizing only the names of persons and places and the beginnings of verses. The romanization and punctuation of song texts in the Sixth View are those of the books from which they are derived. The text of *Shakkyō* was translated by John R. Mayer, that of *Kanda matsuri* by George Gish, Jr., and that of *Hōrai* by David Hughes. Translations of other materials were done by John R. Mayer and edited by the author.

Except for the examples from the score of Benjamin Britten's *Curlew River*, all Western notations and transcriptions were done by the author and copied by Jim Needles. In shamisen notation, the Japanese convention is followed of using the pitch B for the lowest open string without regard to the pitch of the actual performance. The following performance symbols are used for the shamisen:

- ∨   upstroke
- ∩   pizzicato
- ⌒   finger hammer on
- -   finger slide

In *ko tsuzumi* notation the following symbols are used:

×	the sound *pon*
⊏	the sound *chi*
⊐	the sound *pu*
•	the sound *ta*

If an example can be heard on the book cassette, an asterisk appears in the text. If the example is also notated, the specific cassette location is given in the example caption.

PRELUDE

When I received the invitation to be an Ernest Bloch Professor at Berkeley I felt a true sense of honor and privilege. As I then studied the publications that have resulted from the lectures of earlier holders of this chair, I sensed not only a challenge but also some pangs of inadequacy. Nevertheless, it is a great joy for me to present this series of studies, especially in the Bloch centenary year. The series combines nostalgia with an Asian sense of time. Let me explain.

First, there is a high-school memory of listening to Bloch's Concerto Grosso on a new, magical recording machine called a wire recorder. This World War II invention was soon replaced by the tape recorder, but the impressions of the composition that I first heard upon a wire recorder have remained with me to this day. At that time, my reaction to the composition was such that it became my goal to compose like Ernest Bloch, with a little help from the styles of Hindemith, Ravel, and the dance-band arrangements of Woody Herman. Fortunately for future audiences and historical musicologists, I developed very good compositional taste: after a master's degree in composition and a fleeting career as a composer for modern dance, I stopped composing. I left the piano, took up the typewriter, and was able to pursue a more viable occupation. Still, Bloch was one of the first composers to move me towards a musical career, so now, in my seniority period, I find the presentation of these studies in his name and honor to be, for me, most moving and most appropriate. I can only hope that the results will be acceptable as a memorial to such a fine musician and teacher.

The second special meaning of this opportunity to me is its location. I first saw San Francisco in 1947, when I was Mas Malm, the one-man gamelan accompaniment for the Devi Dja Java-Bali Dance Troupe. We played in the Marine Memorial Theater. As I recall we got a good review. My next big moment in San Francisco occurred in the summer of 1959, when John May, through the kind efforts of his sister, Dr. Elizabeth May Slater, lent me his home in the Twin Peaks area. There I was able to write my Ph.D. thesis on Japanese *nagauta* while watching the fog roll in over the Golden Gate Bridge as in some modern version of a Japanese scroll painting. It was in those 1957–59 UCLA graduate years that first Professor David Boyden of the Music Department and then Professor Donald Shively of the Japanese language program invited me to lecture on Japanese music on the campus of the University of California, Berkeley.

So here I am again, some twenty-two years later, back on the same campus speaking on the same topic. The facilities and the faculty are mostly new, and hopefully the content of my lectures will be different as well. Still, I am struck by the fact that 1980 is thirty-three years after my first California experience and twenty-two years after my first lecture at Berkeley. Now, any Asian numerologist would point out that the number thirty-three could be six times five plus three, and twenty-two is three times five plus seven—all auspicious Japanese numbers. I hope they augur well for the lecture series.

The above paragraphs are a transcription of my opening speech on April 14, 1980, in the Wheeler Auditorium of the Music Department of the University of California, Berkeley. I hope that they provide a background for the following studies and establish the mood in which they were originally presented.

It is important that I explain the title of this book. Westerners have always been intrigued by the "mysteries" of Asia. However, the word *hidden* in the title does not necessarily mean something secret in the world of Japanese music. Rather it refers to sets of procedures within that tradition that are so "natural" that many excellent Japanese authors and musicians tend not to speak of them. The word *views* was selected in the spirit of those sets of Japanese wood-block prints that reveal different sides of the same scene, such as Mount Fuji. The choice of a mountainous analogy is deliberate, for Japanese music does loom large, beautiful, and multifaceted on the horizon of my musical world. My basic goal here is merely to share some of this panorama with others. The scenes may be obvious to some Japanese, but they are seen here from a Westerner's point of view and in a Western language. I can only hope that they are a compliment, and not a distortion of the views of Japan's professional musicians. They, after all, really know the secrets. It is in view of this fact that this book is dedicated to my drum teacher, Tanaka Denzaemon XI.

June 1984
WPM

The Art of Ko Tsuzumi Drum Making

Oᴜʀ ꜰɪʀꜱᴛ ᴠɪᴇᴡ of Japanese music is organological, that is, a study in the science of musical instruments. Our specific topic is the *ko tsuzumi* (the "small" *tsuzumi*), an hourglass-shaped drum with two lashed heads, held on the right shoulder by the left hand and struck on the front head by the right hand. The ko tsuzumi and its larger partner, the *ō tsuzumi*, form the core of percussion music in the noh and kabuki theaters.[1]

HISTORY AND SOURCES

The term *tsuzumi* may be derived from the name of an ancient Indian drum, the *dudumbhi*.[2] The characters with which this term can be written are found in Chinese sources that predate Japanese written history.[3] These characters are later found in Japan's first written sources, the eighth-century *Kojiki* and *Nihon shoki*, but neither of these sources seems to refer to an instrument like the tsuzumi of this study.[4] Rather they refer to a larger hourglass-shaped drum held or placed in front of the player and struck on both ends, often using at least one stick. Such drums are found on artifacts and mentioned in documents of continental East Asia and are used in surviving performance forms such as Korean *changko* drumming and the *komagaku* repertory of Japanese *gagaku* court music, in which the lead drum is called the *san no tsuzumi*.[5] However, if the drum under discussion has continental roots, they would seem to be in the street entertainments imported from Korea and China rather than in the courtly traditions.[6] By the thirteenth century we find Japanese equivalents of continental theatricals in such forms as *kusemai* and *shirabyōshi* as well as *dengaku* and *sarugaku*, in all of which the ko tsuzumi seems to be used as the major percussion accompaniment.[7] These various forms contributed to the growth of noh drama in the fourteenth century, which in turn influenced the growth of kabuki drama in the seventeenth century. Throughout all these developments, the ko tsuzumi seems ever present. Thus, the need for ko tsuzumi makers has been part of Japan's organological history for centuries.

This study will be restricted to the making of ko tsuzumi in their present-day form. It is based for the most part on two sources: first, the author's experience in the field of Japanese drumming and conversations with its practitioners and, second, documents on drum making as collected by Ikuta Shigeru and Yamazaki Gakudō in a book published in 1917 on the evaluation of tsuzumi bodies.[8] Ikuta was an executive in the Asahi Beer Company who, like many of the rising financial aristocrats of the time, cultivated intellectual-cultural interests along with business acumen. Ikuta's major artistic efforts seem to have been the study of drumming for the noh drama and, contiguous with that, the collecting of excellent drums. Yamazaki Seitarō, later Gakudō (1885–1944), was the son of a former retainer of the feudal lord of Kii (now Wakayama).[9] His father had studied *kyōgen*, the comic interludes of noh. The son continued this interest with lessons in noh singing (Kita school) and drum playing (Kado school). At the same time he completed a degree in architecture at Tokyo University (1909). Thus, while his profession was architecture, he also became well known as a writer of reviews and general

articles concerning noh. For such writings he used the personal name
Gakudō, which means a hall or temple of pleasure or of music, as in
the word for noh music (*nōgaku*). Under the pen name of Sakamoto
Uchō, he helped publish the basic songbooks for the Kanze and
Umewaka schools of noh. His research writings include studies of
instrument and theater construction, and he actually designed noh
stages. Thus he was an ideal companion for Ikuta in the creation of
this important document.

The book that these men wrote is divided into three sections,
each with separate chapters and pagination. Thus, in our study, page
numbers in references to Ikuta and Yamazaki's book will be as they
actually appear. The first section consists of Ikuta's general description of the parts of a ko tsuzumi drum, with an emphasis on those
features that are significant in the evaluation of an instrument. The
second section is a reproduction of seven privately owned manuscripts on drums and drum makers. The final section is a discussion
by Yamazaki of the genealogy of drum makers. The book also includes Yamazaki's large genealogical chart and a map of the locations
of famous drum makers' shops in the Nara area.

Before we begin our own study of drum making, it is important
to identify briefly the seven manuscripts compiled in Ikuta and
Yamazaki's book:

1. "Dō meikan," "Signature patterns on drum bodies"
2. "Kyōjiki-shō," "A summary of repair handicrafts"
3. "Sandō hishō," "A secret treatise on three drum-body
    makers"
4. "Sekiguchi ike koteki kan," "Remnants of Sekiguchi's
    manuscript 'Drum and flute examples'"
5. "Dō mekiki kōki," "Research records on judging drum
    bodies"
6. "Ko tsuzumi dōshimei oyobi kaname heidō no sunpō,"
    "Master ko tsuzumi drum-body makers and measure-
    ments of drum incisions and bodies"
7. "Kandō yōryaku," "The essentials of drum-body appre-
    ciation"

The sources of these manuscripts were as follows:

1. A family manuscript of Ōnishi Kanestsu, Ikuta's drum
    teacher.

2, 3. Manuscripts owned by Iwata Yoshimichi, proprietor of the Rigan-dō shop (a musical instruments store?) near the Gion shrine in Kyoto. A copy of "Kyōjiki-shō" was also in the collection of a *nagauta* genre ko tsuzumi drummer, Kuni Shinsaburo.

4. A manuscript from the collection of Satake Shōkeidō, owner of a musical instruments store near the Tsūbukkō temple in Tera-machi, Kyoto. Satake's heirs continue the store but in a new location. (Sekiguchi has yet to be identified, though the manuscript is dated 1845–46.)

5. A manuscript from the private collection of Ōkura Hanjiro, a professional noh drummer.

6. A manuscript with copies in the collections of the drummers Ōkura and Kuni.

7. A manuscript owned by Yamazaki's late father.

The compilation of such rare manuscripts in one publication is an organological document of considerable importance.[10] The book is further enhanced by Yamazaki's genealogical efforts and by Ikuta's well-organized presentation of much technical information. Together with this author's own experience, these writings form the basis for our preliminary study. Its purpose is to increase our understanding and appreciation of the ways in which skilled Japanese instrument makers produce ko tsuzumi that are of beautiful appearance and, more important, of beautiful tone.

THE INSTRUMENT

First let us look at the instrument as a whole as shown in Figure 1. The two heads (*kawa*) are lashed to the hourglass-shaped body (*dō*) by some 4.5 meters of rope called the *tateshirabe*.[11] Another 4 meters of rope called the *yokoshirabe* encircle the lashing rope so that the left hand may vary the lashing rope's pressure. Both sets of rope are made of hemp and are some 6 to 7 millimeters thick. Normally their color is a reddish orange, though, since the Edo period (1615–1868), the color purple is allowed for certain distinguished performers. There is, in addition, a darker-colored, small *kojime* line from one lashing hole of the front drumhead to the encircling ropes. A drummer

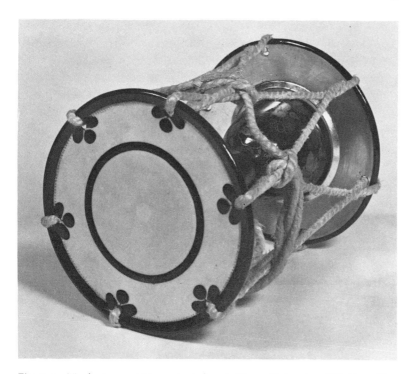

Figure 1. The ko tsuzumi (the author's drum). Photo: University of Michigan Photographic Service.

places the little finger of his left hand in this loop to stabilize his grip. There may also be a green-colored, 2-meter *shimeo* rope that a drummer may tie around the drum while it is resting in order not to lose the degree of tension already set on the drum before a performance. This tension and the skills of the performer are important elements in the tone of a drum, but our concern here is primarily the physical requirements of the drum, starting with the heads.

The heads of the ko tsuzumi are generally 20 centimeters in diameter and made of horsehide wrapped around an iron ring (*fuchi*) and sewn to itself by stitches at the inner side of the ring (*sentōchi*) and in a circle (*bumawashi*) 11 centimeters from the center. The iron ring may first be encased in cherry bark, perhaps to reduce wear. As seen in Figure 2, six holes are provided for the lashing rope. The outer and inner stitches are covered with black lacquer, and a lacquer flower design (*hanagata*) adorns each hole. The backs of the heads are built up with clay lips (*koshigi*) so that the heads may rest firmly on the two cups of the body.

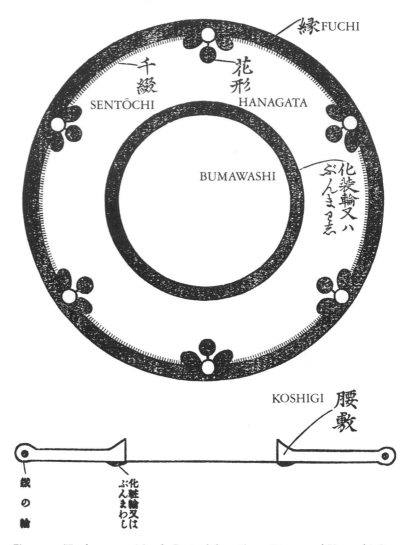

Figure 2. The ko tsuzumi head. Derived from Ikuta Shigeru and Yamazaki Gakudō, *Tsuzumi dō no kantei* (Tokyo: Wanya, 1917), sec. 1, p. 60.

Heads vary in thickness, the struck head (*uchikawa*) often being slightly thinner than the rear head (*uragawa*). Thin heads vibrate more easily but also wear out more quickly and are more sensitive to dampness.[12] An important factor affecting tone quality is a small circle of deerskin that is placed in the back of the struck head. To produce a "proper" tone one or more layers of special tuning paper (*chōshigami*) are placed on the outside of the back head. This paper comes in strips some 1 centimeter wide and is attached by dampening it with the tongue, tearing off small squares, and pressing the squares to the head or to the previous layer(s) of paper. The paper's function is to establish a balance of vibrations between the two heads. The choice of heads by a performer is an extremely personal matter, for the sonic features of each body and each set of heads are different. It is their particular combination that creates tone quality.

What constitutes a "correct" tone is as nebulous and as important as are similar questions concerning a fine Western instrument. We must not lose sight of the fact that the major concern of all good artisans is to make an instrument that will be sturdy and also produce a good tone. In the case of the ko tsuzumi there are four basic sounds on the drum, known onomatopoeically as *ta*, *chi*, *pu*, and *pon*. The manner in which they are played is discussed in the next chapter. Let us look here at ways in which ko tsuzumi tones are judged and then search for the structural aspects of the drum that contribute to such tones.

The nature of the sound pon on a ko tsuzumi seems to be the best means of judging the drum's quality. One can speak of the manner in which the sound "hums" or "buzzes" (*unari*) or comment on the "wave" or "flutter" (*nabiki*) of the sound. However, the "trailing tone" (*yoin*) is considered to be of particular importance. It is said that when a pon is struck, the first 10 percent of the sound (*on*) is the striking and the remaining 90 percent the trailing tone. One may say that a sound is strong (*ōne*) or soft (*kone*) and that the trailing tone is long or short. In addition, the overall sound may seem to expand or be more confined, and it may come to the *n* of the pon or seem to remain open at the end. Figure 3 shows the way in which Ikuta tried to represent graphically this concept of the tone shapes of pon.[13]

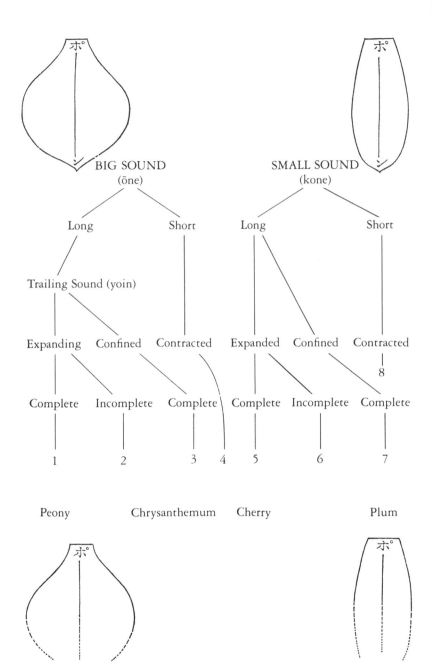

Figure 3. Ko tsuzumi tone qualities. Derived from Ikuta Shigeru and Yamazaki Gakudō, *Tsuzumi dō no kantei* (Tokyo: Wanya, 1917), sec. 1, p. 49.

Ikuta took the concept of tone a step further, as shown in Figure 3. He has attempted to indicate all the combinations possible in a pon tone of a ko tsuzumi. Styles 4 and 8 are rejected because of their extreme shortness, and 6 and 2 are called "distracted and frivolous." The remaining four styles are described in the following fashion:

1. colorful excellence and grace—a tree peony
3. simple and dimly captivating—a chrysanthemum
5. faintly graceful with its luster melting—a cherry blossom
7. simple and mysterious (*yūgen*)—a plum blossom

Ikuta carries the flower analogies further: "Basically it is a matter of choice whether one will love peonies, admire chrysanthemums, pluck off a cherry blossom, or hold aloft a plum blossom. It is fitting that each person should select a blossom according to his own interests of the moment and the general scheme he prefers. However, some of the flowers may have thorns, while others may contain poison. Unfortunately, because they are flowers, one cannot touch them with one's hands."[14]

To some, Ikuta's classifications of tone quality and his comments on it may seem rather fanciful, but actually specificity fails in this aspect of musical instrument making. Ikuta has recognized the subtle but vital distinctions that the musician and the maker must make in order to produce sounds that are aesthetically pleasing to both performer and listener. In the case of the ko tsuzumi we have yet to discuss the very root and stem of this musical flower, the hourglass-shaped body of the drum.

At first glance the art of making a ko tsuzumi body seems to be in the lacquer work. Indeed, art connoisseurs may be more familiar with tsuzumi from museum displays than from their use in noh or kabuki performances. Such external designs are truly beautiful, and the knowledge of their existence on an instrument does add a special ambience to a performer's world. Note, however, that all this artwork is not visible to the performer or the listener once the instrument is picked up and used. Thus, we must turn to the wood itself for the secrets of the tsuzumi's sonic beauty.

The preferred wood for ko tsuzumi making is cherry.[15] The wood must be properly dried before the basic block is cut.[16] Once carved out, the total length of a tsuzumi body (*dō*) is 25 to 27 centimeters and the bowls (*wan* or *uke*) are 8 to 10 centimeters deep.[17] The connecting cylinder (*su*) is 9 to 10.5 centimeters long. The openings at each end of the body generally have an external diameter close to 10 centimeters in order to hold the drumheads snugly. The internal diameter varies according to the shape of the bowl and the thickness of the walls of the cup, and since the better drums are handmade, the openings seldom form perfect circles. A personal survey of tsuzumi bodies has revealed a great variety in the sizes of each part of the drum, particularly in the sixteenth- and early-seventeenth-century versions.

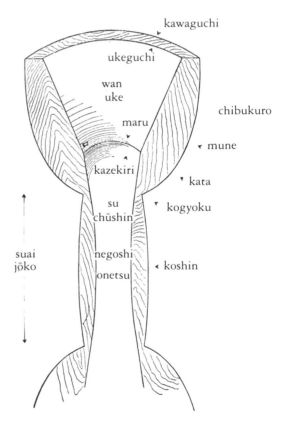

Figure 4. Names of the sections of the ko tsuzumi body. Derived from Ikuta Shigeru and Yamazaki Gakudō, *Tsuzumi dō no kantei* (Tokyo: Wanya, 1917), sec. 1, p. 7.

The various parts of the drum are described in the terms shown in Figure 4. Looking at the external features of the drum first, one finds that the surface where the heads are set is called the mouth for the heads (*kawaguchi*). The "breast pouch" (*chibukuro*) has shoulders (*kata*) and a chest (*mune*). The cylinder is generally called the breeding place (*suai*), though the term *archlike* (*jōko*) is used occasionally because of the convex shape of the external wall of the cylinder. The midpoint of that wall is then called the heart of the arch (*koshin*), and the "arch ends" (*kogyoku*) occur where the cylinder meets the cups.

Looking now at the internal features of the drum, one sees that the bowl has a mouth (*ukeguchi*, literally "a mouth with a protruding lower lip"). The "circle" (*maru*) where the bowl and tube meet is a "wind-cutting" (*kazekiri*) edge. The length of the tube from this edge to that of the other bowl is the "nest" (*su*) or "central heart" (*koshin*) of the drum. If the diameter of the tube is smaller at the center than at the bowls, this point is called the place where the sound comes across (*negoshi* or *onetsu*).

Since the body's function is to transfer and shape the sound waves moving from the front head to the rear, the design of its internal structure is of particular importance. First, there is the shape of the walls of the bowl between the mouth and the kazekiri edge.[18] It may be convex, concave, or at a straight angle. A convex bowl is said to have been used in some ancient drums to produce a strong sound,[19] but the author has never seen or heard such a drum. Concave walls are said to produce a lighter sound, whereas a straighter angle is felt to be best for a strong sound. However, other aspects of the internal structure of the body may affect the quality of the sound. Among them is the internal diameter of the tube. As noted above, it may decrease towards the center of the tube. This may be accomplished by two slightly angled straight lines rising from the kazekiri and extending to the tube center or by a gentle swelling. The latter is more common. In addition, the kazekiri itself may be angular or quite rounded, although moderate smoothing between these two extremes is felt to be a feature by which one can judge the possibility of a good tone on an instrument. However, each maker is capable of combining all these various design elements in a manner that will produce a sound suitable to his own taste and that of the drum guild that prefers his instruments.

The depth of the bowls, the angles of their sides, and the length of the tube influence the distance and thickness of the wood at the two vital points where the cups and cylinder meet on the outside (kogyoku) and the bowls and tube meet on the inside (kazekiri). For the sake of durability under the pressure of hitting the drumhead and tightening the ropes, these points cannot be at the same place. Their placement may influence the tone of the instrument, though no professional comment on this matter has been found so far.

There is yet another factor in tsuzumi body making that often becomes the most notable mark of a particular maker. It is the style and placement of *kaname* (or *kana*), delicate incisions made in the surface of the bowl or tube. Makers and performers both consider these marks as important aspects of a good drum.[20] They also evoke considerable interest among collectors, for they often help to identify the provenance of a drum. The collecting of drum bodies, like that of other art objects, has been an avocation of many rich or aristocratic connoisseurs. Thus it is not always possible to determine whether a maker was designing his incisions for collectors or for performers. Both goals will become apparent with a brief survey of the variety of incision styles used.

The tool used to make kanname in traditional shops is a *nata*. It looks like a miniature hatchet or butcher knife and is used with both knife- and chisel-like motions. The cut marks (*jingon*) are made in the bowl upward, away from the vital edge where the bowl and tube meet. Perhaps the most striking quality of these cuts is their delicacy. They are seen on a rather polished or smooth surface (*magakiji*).[21] They may appear inside the bowl, near the kazekiri, inside the tube, or in a combination of these locations. There are dozens of different styles, and the terms used to describe them vary from one maker to another. Therefore, we shall limit this discussion to only a few of the more common or distinctive styles,[22] some of which are seen in Figure 5. The centipede (*mukade*) incisions may appear singly as a signature or be scattered (*chirashi*) incisions for the sake of style or sound. Parallel scratches in horizontal lines around the inside of the bowl or in rows of short, vertical cuts can be called basic incisions (*dan kaname*).[23] There is great variety in the density of such cuts and the fineness of the lines. Lines in an X form (*katakiri* or *sujichigai*) seem to be deeper cuts. Longer, thin hairlines (*sesaki*) can be combined in many forms, including "crossing-line" patterns (*chigai ke*) or many "longer lines" (*tatesuji* or *tate ke*). If the lines are dense enough they are called ten thousand lines (*senkin* or *bankin*), spring rain (*samidare*), drizzle (*kosame*), or some other fanciful name. A pattern in short, scattered lines is sometimes called *makuzu*, a word derived from the name of an arrowroot vine (*kuzu*) that grows commonly in southern Japan. The name of the *higaki* pattern refers to the branches of cypress trees. There are some patterns such as the chain-shaped cut (*nawame*) that seem to be used primarily as a signature. Finally, there are patterns that are apparently designed with

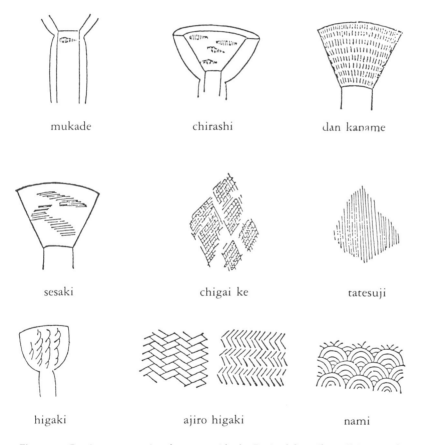

mukade   chirashi   dan kaname

sesaki   chigai ke   tatesuji

higaki   ajiro higaki   nami

Figure 5. Carving patterns in a ko tsuzumi body. Derived from Ikuta Shigeru and Yamazaki Gakudō, *Tsuzumi dō no kantei* (Tokyo: Wanya, 1917), sec. 1, pp. 108–29.

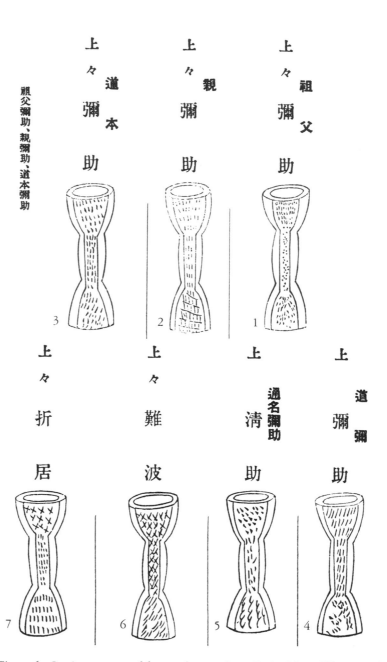

Figure 6. Carving patterns of famous drum makers. Derived from "Ko tsuzumi dōshimei oyobi kaname heidō no sunpō," reproduced in Ikuta Shigeru and Yamazaki Gakudō, *Tsuzumi dō no kantei* (Tokyo: Wanya, 1917), sec. 2, pp. 155–56.

collectors in mind rather than performers. Among these are herring-bone or wickerlike weaving patterns (*ajiro higaki*) as well as actual flower or wave (*nami*) designs. However, the abstract forms and the depth of their cuts seem to be more significant in instruments built for use rather than display. In all, the important point is not so much what an incision pattern is called as that each is in a style known to makers and collectors and therefore is important in the identification of specific instruments.

To illustrate the ways in which the various aspects of ko tsuzumi design are used in the identification of drums, let us look at an excerpt in Figure 6 from a professional source found in Ikuta and Yamazaki's book.[24] The commentary on the drums begins in the upper-right-hand corner and moves across the page, returning to the lower-right-hand corner and crossing to the left again. The first body style discussed is that of the founder of the Yasuke school of drum making. The commentary says that the incisions are thin and cut with the flat side of the groove to the left in the arrowroot-vine design.[25] The walls of the tube and bowl are not thick, and the bowl is swollen, that is, concave. The external curve of the cup is good. The next generation of Yasuke drum makers used the same incision design and produced a good cup shape, but the wall of the tube is more swollen. The lower bowl uses a different style of vine cut. The third drum is by Yasuke Michimoto.[26] He uses similar incisions, but there are slight cross-line patterns in the middle. He also places a signature near the edge of the drum. The cup is less swollen, but the bowl is concave. The first three makers are given the equivalent of two stars for the quality of their work.

The next drum, by Yasuke Dōmi, rates only one star. It has incisions similar to those of other Yasuke instruments, but they seem to be more mixed within one drum. There one may see the cypress, vine, and more scattered patterns (*mekura*, literally "blind"). A disciple of Yasuke Dōmi eventually began to work under the name Tamamoto Kiyosuke.[27] His drum also rates only one star. His incisions are long and narrow, and cypress-branch cuts are also used. The body shape is good, and the walls are thick. The next drum, from the Katanami shop, rates two stars.[28] Its incisions are cross-line, the flat side to the right; a more flowing, vine design is also used. The drums of this shop have a fairly narrow tube, and their walls are somewhat thin. The bowl shapes are good, but highly decorated near the edge, which may be why Katanami drums are judged to be most suitable for someone of the aristocracy. The last drum is from the Orii school, and also rates two stars.[29] It uses cypress-branch designs to the left and right in a style known as the East Peak style (*higashimine*). The name of this style is probably derived from the name of the area where such drums were made. The tube of this drum is straight, and the bowl is not swollen (and therefore perhaps more straight-lined), but the bowl is still deep. The final comment is that there are differing opinions as to which of the Orii shops this drum came from.

This excerpt from a professional document is really only meaningful to someone with a connoisseur's knowledge. However, it is useful to us as an indication of the degree to which technical concerns are a part of the art of Japanese drum making. At the same time it leads us logically to our final and important topic, the drum makers themselves.

In keeping with the traditions of most Japanese arts, the drum makers can be classified as belonging to various guilds or shops. The makers of drums before the flourishing of the ko tsuzumi can be traced to three schools that produced instruments for the court orchestra (gagaku) tradition before the thirteenth century. As seen in Figure 7, these were the Amako, Chine, and Shō guilds. Drum makers established themselves in villages around the tree-filled mountains to the south and west of Nara. Though most shops are now in Kyoto, Tokyo, and other locations, the Nara area is still felt to be the best source of good wood for instrument making. Therefore, let us use the Shō guild from this region as an example of the long lineage of the drum-making tradition.

With the rise of fourteenth-century theatricals both on the streets and in shrines and temples, the need for drum makers increased. Therefore, out of the Shō guild began a new shop, the Shōami, which made tsuzumi rather than court instruments. This shop used cherry wood from the Fukai area in Kita Katsuragi-gun southwest of Nara. Instruments from this shop can be identified not only by their use of Fukai cherry wood but also by their slightly shorter, older

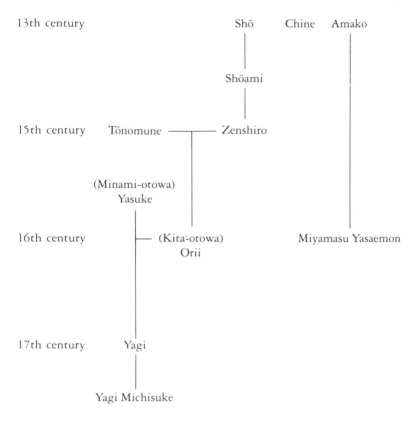

13th century   Shō   Chine   Amako

                                      Shōami

15th century   Tōnomune ————— Zenshiro

                  (Minami-otowa)
                     Yasuke

16th century   ⌐— (Kita-otowa)   Miyamasu Yasaemon
                             Orii

17th century   Yagi

              Yagi Michisuke

Figure 7. A genealogy of drum makers. Derived from a chart accompanying Ikuta Shigeru and Yamazaki Gakudō, *Tsuzumi dō no kantei* (Tokyo: Wanya, 1917).

body styles, their somewhat wide chirashi incision patterns, and their tendency to produce high tones and to work best with thick skins.[30]

In the fifteenth century a member of the third generation of the Shōami family began his own shop under the name Tatsuyoshi Zenshiro. At that time many other drum makers were found in the Mount Tōnomune area, particularly along the Teragawa River near a village appropriately named Cherrywell (Sakurai).[31] The fifteenth-century maker Yasuke Dōkō began a shop in the small village called Minami-otowa; thus either his name or that of his location is used to

identify his drums. By the second generation of this shop, one member had moved slightly north to Kita-otowa and started a new shop
under the name Orii, the name of the nearest village.[32] By the seventeenth century the main Yasuke guild had a shop in the town of Yagi
(now part of the city of Kashihara). Thus one maker identified himself as Yagi Yasuke (d. 1628). This maker later changed his name to
Yagi Michisuke and through his disciples established a new group of
drum makers.

By the eighteenth century Yagi drum shops were found in distant
Edo (Tokyo). Such a move was logical since the kabuki and noh theaters there were customers as important as the theaters of Osaka and
Kyoto. The genealogical chart becomes quite broad with the continual opening of new shops in the Kansai and Kanto regions. Though
the chart in our source ends before the nineteenth century, the tradition does not. Tsuzumi are still made, and spiraling prices imply
that they are still much in demand. Interest in the history of the art
can be observed in the commentaries of professional performers and
owners of major drum stores.

Figure 8. The drum signature of Miyamasu Yasaemon (on the author's drum).
Photo: University of Michigan Photographic Service.

At the oral presentation of this Bloch lecture a drum was used that, at first, seemed to be a possible product of the school that we have just discussed. The name Yasaemon was skillfully written over the striations on the cup, as was an abstract symbol in which was hidden the name of the tradition to which the maker belonged. Later research in Japan revealed that the sounds that were heard at that lecture in fact emanated from a drum signed by Miyamasu Yasaemon sometime between 1573 and 1624 (see Figure 8).[33] Only those in attendance at the lecture can say if the sounds produced were worthy of the rare instrument upon which they were played. What should be clear to the present reader is the impressive past of skilled and sensitive drum makers in Japan. With an appreciation for the art of making such drums we can turn next to a discussion of the way in which one is taught to play them.

Japanese Drum Lessons

AMONG THE SEVERAL DEFINITIONS of the word *lesson* in an English dictionary, one finds such meanings as "a period of instruction" and "an exercise to be studied by a pupil." In the context of learning to play a Western musical instrument, these two aspects of a lesson are combined in the music-educational method called "the lesson plan." In Western pedagogy one can observe the concept of a logical growth of technical skills and musical knowledge. Exercises and graded pieces are well organized to lead the student towards the ultimate goal of musical competence. The choice of particular pieces and exercises can be changed to meet the specific needs of the student, but in Western teaching there generally is a reassuring sense of orderly progress: from simple to complex, from exercise to application. Of course, in all this methodology one must not forget that, under the guidance of a talented teacher, the student may also be informed of the nuances of interpretation that may turn a performance of a piece into something that is not only skilled but also beautiful.

In contemporary Japan, the systematic nature of Western teaching methods has appealed to many teachers of traditional instruments, particularly in the koto and shamisen guilds. At the same time, the Suzuki violin method has become well known in the West for its mixture of Japanese and Western elements of music education and assertive business-industrial know-how. However, I wish to concentrate on rather different lessons: those given on the ko tsuzumi and *taiko* drums to students of the kabuki music tradition. Perhaps by means of this exposition we may be able to see not only another view of Japanese music but also alternative methods and deeper goals in music education. Such a presentation, I feel, is particularly fitting on the occasion of the Bloch centenary. Ernest Bloch certainly was sensitive to alternative solutions to musical problems, to the shaping rather than the destruction of traditional materials, and to the possible spiritual powers of a musical event. Let us turn, then, to the Japanese drum lesson for such insights.

The major source and inspiration for this essay are lessons I received in 1955–57 from Tanaka Denzaemon XI, head of the Tanaka guild of kabuki drummers. I also took festival drum lessons in 1961 from Wakayama Taneo, head of a guild of *Edo bayashi* performers. Finally, I have had some twenty years' experience of field observations and of attempting to teach Japanese drumming to Western students. The presumption of giving those lessons to Western students came to me only late in life. After all, I obtained no professional name (*natori*) while studying in Japan, as my aims then were primarily to use practical experience as an aid in the analysis of Japanese music. Nevertheless, I am grateful for both the Eastern and the Western experiences. Thanks to the traditional nature of my Japanese teachers, my lessons, I think, were "authentic." Thanks to the diligence and, in some cases, the resistance of my American students, I was forced to recognize the logical necessity of using a different, Japanese approach if I wanted to teach Japanese music correctly. I do not claim that the goals of the teaching I am about to describe are uniquely Japanese. It is only that I first perceived them while studying the performance of Japanese music and wish to share them with others in that context. My basic thesis is simple but powerful: a Japanese lesson is ritually and intellectually structured

in such a way that its ultimate goal may be spiritual rather than musical. Such a view of Japanese music does not lend itself easily to
written or verbal description. It involves insight, and insight means,
among other things, looking inside as much as out. Nevertheless, let
us start with written sources, and then move towards the deeper
points.

Until recent times the major source books for kabuki drum music
were actually handbooks for noh drumming.[1] These describe drum
patterns and other technical aspects of playing, but they are not in
lesson form, nor do they discuss means by which their information is
to be passed on to a student. Actual scores for kabuki drum music
are rare. They are written like the later sections of books for noh
drumming: both use columns on grids in which drum parts are notated along with the text of the vocal part and/or the mnemonics of
other instruments if they are used (see Figure 13, p. 45). In noh
drama the only melodic instrument other than the voice is the noh
flute (*nōkan*), and in kabuki one finds the shamisen line.[2] In addition, one may occasionally find a music handbook for kabuki plays
called the *tsukechō*, which indicates where in the text the music is to
enter and what type of music is to be used, though there is no detailed notation of the actual music.

What insights are to be gained from studying these sources? First
one must recognize that Japanese drumming is fundamentally an
oral (though intellectual) tradition. The student memorizes named
drum patterns with diligence and accuracy, and can read in the handbooks about some of the uses of such patterns. However, the written
versions of compositions are never in "full score"; it is not possible to
sight-read them or to observe, on the basis of the printed materials
provided, what the other performers are doing.[3] What should be im-
plicit here is that the basic function of such printed music is to serve
as a memory aid—an aid to recalling what one learns in lessons or in
observations of actual performances. Printed parts or handbooks are,
in fact, not to be used during a lesson at all. One is taught orally and
must come to the next lesson with the previous lesson's materials
memorized. If a student owns printed parts, handbooks, or in modern times a tape recorder, so much the better for private practice,
but drum lessons are to be totally oral except for what can be learned

by watching. Observation is possible since there is no notation to distract the eye. One sees only the teacher or other students; thus all lessons have the aura of a performance.

In speaking of the lessons themselves we should note first that one must develop a patient sense of time. In traditional practice, a music teacher (*sensei*) gives lessons on certain days at certain places but not at a specific time for each student. To take a lesson one simply goes on the right day to the right place and waits. The waiting period equals approximately twenty minutes times the number of students who have arrived earlier, and is usually spent in the lesson room. Thus, one normally cannot rehearse just before a lesson. Rather, the sound and spirit of other players and other compositions permeate the ear and mind before *the* lesson.

Many professional drummers do not have time for extensive teaching, in which case private lessons may be scheduled. Such scheduling is common for lessons given to foreigners, who sometimes have difficulty adjusting to the Japanese concept of time. Even in scheduled lessons, however, a period of nonperformance seems essential to the structure of a lesson. One normally enters a lesson room alone and sits formally facing the art alcove (*tokonoma*) and the wooden block (*hyōshiban*) and leather-covered fans (*haruogi*) that the teacher will use for instruction. In these first moments, one has time to think through the coming lesson, but often the time is used more for absorbing the atmosphere. Sometimes this "activity" is somewhat like the preparations that one makes for a performance; at other times it may be more akin to meditation. If a drum is before one, looking at its shape and lacquer designs can generate what seems to be an exchange of aesthetic goals between the performer and the instrument. It took several years for me to recognize the importance of such nonactive efforts. The insight implied here is, to me, more powerful if it is simply stated, though it is not often simple to achieve: the path towards becoming a good drummer requires that one first become a good drum. I have heard similar statements of intimacy between Western musicians and their instruments, but the rituals towards its accomplishment seem less organized in the West.[4] In both worlds the source of this merger is internal, although a teacher may serve as a guide towards such enlightenment. However, in the West the teacher is primarily a guide towards the spirit of the music, whereas a traditional Japanese teacher is more a guide into a ritual whose goals may differ for different students; some may be musical, some technical, and some spiritual.

When speaking about the spirituality of drum lessons I have encountered people who bring up the frequent use of drums in shamanistic rituals. I do not wish to construe the Japanese drum or its teacher on this level; nor do I wish to romanticize the Japanese artistic world by calling attention to its magic. Nevertheless, one cannot ignore the deeper, nonsonic structure of a Japanese drum lesson without losing what may be its most powerful appeal and its reason for being.

The entrance of the teacher into the room is the first step in the ritual of a drum lesson.[5] In a traditional lesson, the specific forms of bows and verbal expressions that are exchanged are adumbrations of a series of codified gestures and activities that are essential to the goals of drumming. It can be said that, in Japanese music in general, it is not only what you do but also how you do it. In the world of Japanese drumming this attitude may be the secret of the art. Without assuming any mystical pretensions, it might be said that without this basic viewpoint you may perform as a drummer but you cannot become a drum; you have missed the reason for drumming. For further explanation we must turn to the lesson itself.

A preliminary lesson on the ko tsuzumi is concerned with assembling the drum. Of course, certain parts of such an activity are necessary if the drum is to hold together and make a sound. What is perhaps of equal importance, however, is the choreography of the motions that one must execute to assemble a drum correctly. A verbal description of this process would read like an anatomical description of a great moment in dance. Therefore, let us say here merely that the placement of every finger, and the direction and degree of every twist of the hands, are set in such a way that tying the ropes can be as aesthetically pleasing as playing the instrument. If the ropes are tied correctly, the final knot will be in the form of a butterfly. In the theater, this elegant choreography is done before the drummer enters onto the stage. Thus, it cannot be considered theatrical in purpose. We noted in the First View that the exterior of the

drum—with its exquisite lacquer designs—is hidden from an audience once the drummer begins to play. The knot is only partially
visible. What is important, perhaps, is that the drummer and the
enlightened listener know that those things are there, hidden but
beautiful. Of course, it is premature in a lesson to be aware of this
indirect stage effect, but controlled motions towards an aesthetic
event before actually performing have another vital function. Properly executed, they help to make the drummer feel beautiful. As in
most arts, perhaps particularly those of Japan, it is not really possible to create a totally beautiful artistic event if the artist does not
enter into that beauty at the moment it occurs.[6] The word *totally* is
central to the pleasures and challenges of such artistic performance.
But we have yet to pick up the drum.

By now it should come as no surprise to learn that the manner in
which one picks up a drum is equally specific. It should be noted at
this point that different guilds of drummers may use other gestures
throughout the sequence under discussion. What is significant is not
the actual movements but rather the fact that the movements *are*

(a)   (b)

Figure 9. The sitting position of a ko tsuzumi drummer. From Tanaka Denzaemon
XI, *Narimono kyōsokuhon* (Tokyo: Kokuritsu gekijō, 1970), vol. 2, pp. 18 and 20,
courtesy of the National Theater of Japan.

specific and can create analogous internal and external results. Figure 9a shows the ideal sitting position of a Tanaka guild drummer on a kabuki stage.[7] First, note the closed fan set to the left of the musician. The drummer carefully removes the fan from his waistband once he is seated in the proper formal position shown. The rear head of the drum faces the audience. At a specific moment in a composition, the left hand picks up the drum and places it on the left side of the lap with the rear head facing to the right (Figure 9b). At yet another specific moment the drum is raised slowly to the right shoulder. The illustrations in Figure 10, with their carefully drawn lines, are in the spirit of modern teaching, but the angles and proportions shown are in fact consonant with those that one can observe in the theater or in photographs or drawings of earlier kabuki ensembles.[8] Note how the arm motions are considered with equal seriousness. Little of this information, however, is directly taught in music lessons after the preliminary ones. In early lessons the teacher

Figure 10. The ko tsuzumi playing position and movements. From Tanaka Denzaemon XI, *Narimono kyōsokuhon* (Tokyo: Kokuritsu gekijō, 1970), vol. 2, pp. 20, 30, and 31, courtesy of the National Theater of Japan.

may hold a drum so that the student can observe the motions that make for a beautiful sound correctly executed. One's own efforts may evoke a comment of good or bad, but seldom is there any verbal guidance as to how to improve or maintain the sounds created. Before we actually produce a sound on a drum, however, let us turn to yet another instrument, the taiko stick drum.

The tying together of this drum is equally filled with loving details; the opening of the wooden stand upon which it rests has always represented to me an ingenious combination of choreography and carpentry. What may be most germane to the present topic is the art of picking up the taiko drumsticks (*bachi*). They rest on the stand below the drum. As seen in Figure 11, the sticks are not held in the same manner in each hand. The fingers of the right hand are above the stick, the thumb and forefinger holding it in suspension. The left hand is rolled over so that a similar but opposite position cradles the other stick. The drummer must pick up the sticks in such a way

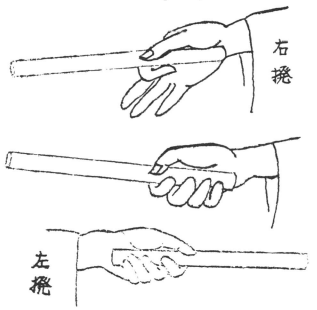

Figure 11. Taiko hand positions. From Tanaka Denzaemon XI, *Narimono kyōsokuhon* (Tokyo: Kokuritsu gekijō, 1970), vol. 1, p. 18, courtesy of the National Theater of Japan.

that they will rest on his legs with the hands in the proper positions. There are at least two manners of doing this (depending on the guild to which one belongs), and it may take some time before one can do it properly. Once it is done correctly, however, one is ready to strike the drum.

Though the cowhide head of the taiko is generally 35 centimeters in diameter, it is struck only in one, 5-centimeter spot in the center. Over this spot is placed a patch of deerskin. Its function is to deaden slightly the tone of the drum, to give it that *shibui* quality of non-specificity so well known in other Japanese arts.[9] In a traditional taiko lesson, one first experiences what seems to be a rare example of warm-up exercises in Japanese music. The small, medium, and large drum strokes (*sho*, *chū*, and *dai*) are played first with the right stick and then with the left. However, further detail is required. After playing three small strokes the stick returns silently to the drumhead. A similar silent motion follows each of the following sequences of three strokes. Ritually the total movement contains an auspicious number of strokes (3 × 3 = 9) plus the slow, silent motions of the sticks. By the time the entire ritual has been completed each stick and its arm are fused into one physical, sound-producing unit. At that moment the mind and body are almost ready to play a drum pattern. However, there is yet the challenge of placing both sticks on the drumhead. To do this successfully the drum must be at such a distance from the drummer's body that both arms are rounded and not angular, as seen in Figure 12a.[10] Again, the function of these preliminary gestures seems to be to assist the drummer to enter into a state of being beautiful. It is at this moment that one may learn a drum pattern. Usually it is *kizami*, as shown in Example 1. The pattern consists of unaccented pulses made distinct within an eight-beat frame (*yatsubyōshi*) only by the interjection of three vocal drum calls (*kakegoe*). *Kizami* means to cut, chisel, or notch, and one can certainly hear a fine cutting of the eight beats into smaller units. It is the most common pattern in taiko music, but it is not our purpose here to discuss its musical functions.[11] In the context of early lessons, kizami plays an important nonmusical role; it helps the performer become two drumsticks. If the ko tsuzumi player must have no hand, then the taiko player must have no arms. Analogies in the art

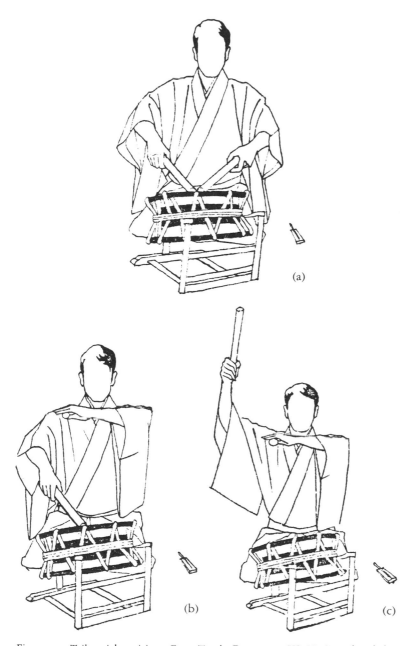

Figure 12. Taiko stick positions. From Tanaka Denzaemon XI, *Narimono kyōsokuhon* (Tokyo: Kokuritsu gekijō, 1970), vol. 1, pp. 50–51, courtesy of the National Theater of Japan.

of Japanese painting come immediately to mind.[12] Until the arm and
the art-producing instrument become one, the work of art will not
emerge.

Example 1. The taiko pattern kizami.

Once one has a feel for the art of the kizami pattern, other, more
involved patterns are taught that use different-sized strokes and
rhythmic changes. Finally, the student is allowed to try the cadence
pattern *kashira*. Its physical challenges are formidable. The two
sticks rise suddenly from the drumhead only to reverse direction, the
right stick touching the head (silently) at the moment the left stick
reaches the right shoulder (see Figure 12b). During all this motion a
forceful "ho" drum call has begun, but it changes to a falsetto sound
at the moment the right stick begins to rise towards its highest position (Figure 12c). Once it reaches this point, the left stick flashes out
from the right shoulder to strike the head and generate a totally different "iya" drum call, whose conclusion is followed by the descending stroke of the right stick. After twenty-five years of observation, I
never cease to thrill at the choreographic wonder of the kashira. Its
proper rendition involves more than the physical motions described;
the player must feel beautiful enough to be able to play grandly. It is
not merely a matter of practice; it is a gathering and then releasing
of spirit.

If one has mastered basic patterns and their technical complex-
ities, it is possible to play an entire composition by memorizing the
order of the patterns in it. However, there are still other lessons to be
learned. First, there is the search for beat 1. What seems (to most
Western ears at least) to be the first beat of a taiko drum pattern is
marked as beat 2 in the drum books. When these patterns are performed with a full ensemble the discrepancy between the various
lines seems even more confusing.[13] At this point one needs to meditate further on the final cadence pattern, kashira. It means the head,

not the end, and ends on beat 1, not beat 8. Next a drum student discovers that the distance (*ma*) between the beats of patterns so carefully learned is not always the same. It seems that knowledge is never what one expects.

Let me turn, in this connection, to enlightenments that came to me from my experience in learning to play Edo festival music (*matsuri bayashi*). Each week I would meet with my teacher, Wakayama Taneo, across a table in his room, where he would beat out the rhythmic patterns of the instruments with fans while I repeated them with my hands. All this was done with sung mnemonics (not notation) for support. When I had learned the parts for the two drums, the small gong, and eventually the flute of the five basic pieces,[14] my lessons were over. I left for America. Throughout that experience I never played one percussion instrument and therefore obviously never played any of the parts in an actual ensemble. However, the Stearns Collection of Musical Instruments of the University of Michigan generously purchased a complete set of the instruments required for the festival music, so I formed a group at the university and passed on all the mnemonics and performance gestures that I had learned or observed in my teacher's room or at a festival. Thus, my debut as a performer of Edo matsuri bayashi was in Ann Arbor, Michigan. The performance seemed to work, but I was frustrated at the time by the fact that there was no recording by my teacher's guild that I could use for guidance. It always seemed to be my fate that my teachers in any genre did not belong to the schools that appeared on commercial records. This was particularly irritating because the recorded performances of pieces I knew did not seem to be the same as what I had learned. Imagine, then, my excitement when a record arrived from Japan that contained performances by my teacher's ensemble of all the compositions I had been taught. What did I find? That the recorded music was also different from what I had learned. I was shocked and upset. My first thoughts were of archaic feudalism, in which guild secrets are essential to socioeconomic control. After all, one is always seeing in old Japanese books references to "secret pieces" (*hikyoku*). There is even the anomaly of notations of secret pieces.[15] Eventually two other thoughts arose. First, I began to see a logic in controlling the performance of "real" pieces so that only someone capable of playing them correctly can actually do so. If one were to walk down the hallway of the practice rooms of any Western music school, the distortions of great Western works, locked in their Gutenberg prisons of detailed notation, would become most evident. From a pragmatic standpoint perhaps the nonexistence or indefinite nature of Japanese notation may help to control who plays what, and when.

The second thought that occurred to me is more germane to the subject of this essay. Perhaps I was experiencing something very common in the lives of Buddhist novitiates or, for that matter, of Western graduate students. I recognized at last that what one learns is not the truth . . . but that one cannot find the truth without it.

Where does all this nondirection lead us? I can only imply an answer by referring finally to my experience in teaching Western students to play Japanese music. After years of trying to explain *how* to play a ko tsuzumi or a taiko I began to find that there was an inverse ratio between instruction and learning. The less I said about how to play something, the better progress the student would make. If I only said to the ko tsuzumi student, "You have no hand," the player often improved, and admonitions towards beauty made a more successful taiko player than analyses of the movements. At the same time the ritual motions of the lessons and performances seemed to absorb both the teacher and the performer into a state of complete seriousness and brilliant nonintellectualization.[16] Finally, let me recall a very skilled and eager young composer who wanted to learn to play the taiko. The speed of his learning was impressive, but at the end of the first lesson I could not teach him kashira. I was restrained by the feeling that he was not spiritually ready for it. Because of the respect I bore him, I taught him kashira at a later, more spiritually viable time.

I first experienced Japanese music in situ in 1955. Shortly afterward I took the assertive course of action proper to Western youth and wrote about it. In later years the inflexibility of those early printed words has remained to confound and embarrass me.[17] However, in searching quite blindly at that time for some kind of clever opening for the book, I found a section of a poem by Zenji Hakuin that mentioned music, "Utau mo mau mo, nori no koe," and translated it as

Both music and dance
Are voices of the Way.

Now I might use "Utau mo mau mo, michi no nori," and translate it
as

Both song and dance,
Paths of the Way.

One path is in the art of drumming.

General Principles of Japanese Music

Oᴜʀ ꜰɪʀsᴛ ᴛᴡᴏ ᴠɪᴇᴡs of Japanese music have dealt with drum construction, evaluation, and teaching. Since the remaining four will concentrate on music, we should first become familiar with some of the technical terms and fundamental characteristics of Japanese music, particularly as they are reflected in noh and the nagauta genre of shamisen music, for these are the major genres from which our examples will be drawn. This interlude is meant to provide the reader with a general background for the topics to be discussed and thus is selective, not comprehensive. After a brief survey of the noh and shamisen music I shall discuss more theoretical topics. Subheadings will help readers to choose areas in which they may wish additional information now or later in the studies. I hope that this structure will keep important but distracting details from disturbing the flow of the analytical materials that lie ahead.

NOH MUSIC

Specific musical details concerning noh will emerge as needed during the studies.[1] At this point it is sufficient to say that noh music consists of the chanting of actors (the *shite*, *waki*, and subsidiary characters) and a unison chorus (*ji*). Such chanting may or may not be accompanied by members of the instrumental ensemble collectively known as the *hayashi*, which consists of a flute (nōkan) and the three drums discussed in the previous chapters (the taiko stick drum and the ō and ko tsuzumi hand drums). The general terms for noh chanting are *yōkyoku* and *utai*. The rules for the melodic and rhythmic shapes of noh chanting are many and specific.[2] However, one must be prepared to find differences in the way particular guilds and individuals interpret these rules.

Form in noh music is naturally shaped by the needs of a given drama. Large or small units of noh are frequently discussed in terms of the tripartite division *jo ha kyū* (introduction, scattering, rushing). Specific sections of noh form will be identified as needed in our analyses. Perhaps the most useful general comment to be made at this point is that the conventions of order in noh form and of the types of music that are appropriate to each section are important "hidden," that is, covert, clues that help a listener sense the forward progression in a composition.[3]

NAGAUTA

The standard nagauta ensemble consists of singers, an equal number of shamisen, and the hayashi ensemble of the noh. The flute player often doubles on the bamboo flute (*takebue* or *shinobue*). Since nagauta music originated in the kabuki theater, many offstage (*geza*) instruments may be used as well.[4] Such additions are usually inspired by meanings in the text or its mood. The jo ha kyū terminology of noh is used in modern nagauta studies as well. Modern Japanese scholarship has also coined the term *kabuki dance form* to provide a basis for analyzing the structure of individual pieces. The six basic sections of the form are the *oki*, *michiyuki*, *kudoki*, *odori ji*, *chirashi*, and *dangire* (or *dangiri*). These sections are often identifiable by conventions of style or orchestration.[5] The same is true for many

sections in a noh drama. Such tendencies are important to both traditions since their music is through-composed; that is, the progression from one section of a piece to the next is not based on tonal or
thematic relations. There are no first or second themes that can be
traced throughout a piece as in a Western classical composition.
Thus the sonic clues of sectional change in Japanese music are important to the sense of logical progression through musical time.

TONALITY AND MELODIC TENSION

The roots of Japanese theories of tonal systems are found in Chinese-
inspired tomes on Buddhist or court (gagaku) music. This is evident
in the tonal nomenclature of noh, though its melodic style is quite
different from that of Buddhist or court singing. For example, the
music of the noh flute (nōkan) is considered to be in the ancient
ōshiki-chō mode if pitches produced by right-hand fingerings predominate and in the banshiki-chō (in ancient theory a whole step
higher than ōshiki-chō) if pitches produced by left-hand fingerings
predominate.[6] In vocal music, the central pitches are called by the
old Buddhist music terms low (ge), middle (chū), and high (jo). The
terms for satellite pitches come from the same source and help define
their position in relation to the central pitches.[7] The distances between pitches are determined by the stylistic needs of the text or
melody. In lyrical melodies (yowagin) the three central pitches are a
fourth apart (e.g., F-C-G), whereas strong-style melodies (tsuyōgin)
usually reduce the central pitches to two, sometimes as close as a
minor third.[8]

Tonal theory in noh is not based on pitch or scale in the Western
sense of A 440 or A major. Rather its rules are concerned more with
the distances between central pitches and the gravitation of other
pitches to them. This concept is fundamental to an understanding of
Japanese melodic design in general. Traditional Japanese music is
aharmonic; that is, there are no triadic chords or chord progressions
that may color a melodic line or drive it on in time. These harmonic
functions are important in Western music. Some of these same functions are assumed in Japanese music by rhythmic devices.[9] In terms
of our present topic, however, let us note that in aharmonic music

melodic tension is particularly important. In noh drama, melodic movement to and from pitch centers is quite regulated, and reciting tones above central pitches are common. In the shamisen music that we shall study, melodic tension is created by the use of upper or lower leading tones to a tonal center or its fifth. To understand this further we must turn to the tonal systems of shamisen music.

Before we enter into a discussion of scales, an important visual-sonic caveat is necessary concerning our use of Western notation. There are, of course, logical and flexible forms of traditional notation (see pp. 43–49) that could be used. However, in this book that would be difficult because they differ considerably between genres or instruments and often even between schools within one tradition. Thus, in the interest of continuity and communication, Western notation is used in the transcriptions of scales or melodies throughout the book. We noted earlier (p. xxi) that the Japanese convention of using B for the lowest open string in Western transcriptions of shamisen music will be followed regardless of the pitch of the actual performance. Noh examples are similarly adjusted for comparison's sake. Thus, a reader with so-called perfect (i.e., Western) pitch must be prepared to look at the transcriptions as a kind of movable-*do* system. In addition, the intervals between pitches in both noh and shamisen music are often not those of the Western tempered scale. For example, the distance between an upper leading tone and a pitch center is usually smaller than the Western half step. The basic admonition, then, is not to take the transcriptions literally and, whenever possible, to "correct" them with careful listening to the actual music.

Example 2a shows the traditional two scales common to shamisen and koto music. Their names, *yo* and *in*, relate to dual concepts in ancient Chinese music theory and philosophy. A Western musician can see that these scales are constructed from two tetrachords of four pitches each, making a full octave scale. However, pitches 2 and 3 or 6 and 7 are "changing tones" (*hen-on*, in Chinese *bian yin*): one can be substituted for the other rather than being played one after the other. Thus, actual shamisen music tends to generate pentatonic scales from such seven-tone vocabularies. In recognition of this, contemporary Japanese scholars have envisioned Japanese tonal systems not so much as scales but rather as combinations of tetrachords that consist of two nuclear pitches (*kakuon*) a perfect fourth apart plus *one* intermediate pitch.[10] Example 2b shows the four types of tetrachords presently used in Japanese analysis and writings. They are notated in the pitches in which they are most likely to appear in the transcriptions of this book. The term *minyō* (folk song) is used for the first tetrachord because it is common to that genre. *Miyako* (Kyoto) is used for the second because it is common to the urban music of that

Example 2. Japanese tonal sytems.

world in the Edo period (1615–1868). The term *ritsu* is used for the third because it is the basis of the *ritsu* scale of court music. The fourth tetrachord is called *ryūkyū* because it appears only in the music of the Ryukyu islands; it thus is not germane to our study. With such building blocks one can construct all the scale types of Japan. In Example 2c, one can see two minyō tetrachords used to create what is sometimes known as an *inaka* (country) scale, whereas a combination of two urban tetrachords could be called a miyako scale. One can think modally in these pentatonic scales by using the G in inaka or the A in miyako as the pitch center. These modes are sometimes called *yonanuki* (literally "take out the fourth and seventh [pitches]"). Example 2d shows how common changes in the ascending and descending forms of scales in shamisen music would be represented in the tetrachordal system. Such music may contain sudden modulations. However, there is often very little sonic information with which to judge the tonality of a passage. It is in such situations that a three-tone system is better than a seven-tone one. This tetrachordal approach, along with the concept mentioned earlier of melodic tension engendered by upper and lower leading tones to roots or fifths, will help the reader appreciate the tonal art of the music to be discussed in the studies that follow.

TIME AND RHYTHM

Of the genres discussed in this book, noh drama is the richest in writings on the concept of rhythm. Such publications tend to be more practical than theoretical since they were written in response to the growing market of amateur performers.[11] In the shamisen world, the *gidayū* genre of the puppet theater led to the production of explanatory books for a similar market.[12] However, in general, traditional shamisen musicians have felt no need to produce theoretical books on a music that they personally understand so well "naturally" (*shizen ni*). We noted above that modern Japanese scholars have shown a very different attitude. Perhaps the inroads made in Japan by Western music and Western teaching methods, with all their pedagogical paraphernalia, inspired these Japanese scholars to meet the competition with equivalent publications. Whatever the motivation, our insights have been enriched by such efforts. A good example of this new approach is the twentieth-century explanation of traditional views of meter in Japanese shamisen music.[13]

First, it should be noted that most Japanese music is not meter-oriented. Perhaps the closest one comes to encountering meter is in gagaku court music, which historically is derived from a musical tradition of continental East Asia.[14] In most modern notation of shamisen music, bar lines are used, and that convention is followed here in the use of 2/4-meter transcriptions. However, the implied accents of such metric frames are not natural to traditional Japanese musicians. According to modern Japanese music-theory books the accent in, for example, 2/4 can be either forward (*hyō hyōshi*), on the first beat, or back (*ura hyōshi*), on the second beat. The spirit of relativity once more rises before us. This flexibility is possible because the accents of given Japanese melodic lines are perceived more in the context of entire phrases, independently of any bar lines. This, of course, is not unique to Japan (think of the Western Renaissance). What is significant in Japan is the *non*reference to any metric frame by the traditional musicians themselves.

Japanese percussionists are naturally more articulate than other performers on the topic of rhythm. The concept of named, stereotyped rhythmic patterns (*tetsuke*) is basic to the drum music of the two genres discussed in this book. These patterns are spoken of in the context of an eight-beat frame (yatsubyōshi), though the actual length of the patterns may vary from two to twenty beats. The concept of meter is obviously not relevant to this kind of rhythmic structure. It becomes even less useful when a full hayashi and the shamisen are all playing. As will be shown, the "first beats" of the phrases of these various instruments often do not coincide; internally symmetrical units are begun at different times in a common time frame. In previous years I have called this the slide-rule effect, but the slide rule became circular rather than linear and then was replaced by calculators and computers, so the term has lost its meaning to persons under thirty. While in Japan I thought of a better and perhaps longer-lived term, *sliding-doors effect*. The similarity between sliding doors and Japanese rhythmic structure is as follows. If there are two or more doors in a frame, each has a specific size and each has a track parallel to that of the other doors. However, when doors move along their tracks they may start from different positions. They usually come to an equal, parallel position only at the end of the track (the cadence?). The "sliding," disjunct phrases in Japanese music are one of the hidden devices that contribute to the sense of forward motion in time.

Another rhythmic disjunction is evident if one listens to a singer and shamisen performing together. Though both parts are following the same general melodic line, they seldom change pitches on the same beat. The term *fusoku furi* (neutrality) has been applied to the vocal line,[15] for it often seems to float behind the line of the accompanying shamisen. This practice helps one to hear more clearly the syllables of the text, and also creates another line of rhythmic tension that requires release at the cadence. Since this practice involves simultaneous variations of the basic melody, it might be regarded as a type of heterophony, though, to me, the clarification of the text that it achieves and its rhythmic tension outweigh its melodic differences.[16]

Not all Japanese music is metronomic, nor is it necessarily rhythmically integrated. We shall see several examples of parlando rubato in the chapters ahead. We should note also that in noh a distinction is made between sections in which the voice and drums are rhythmically integrated (*hyōshi ai au* or *awase*) and sections in which they are not (*fuai*). A hidden aspect of time in Japanese music, however, is the concept of ma, the space between events. This concept is well known in most Japanese arts.[17] In music it provides a rhythmic elasticity in which silence is as powerful as sound. Awareness of the art of ma is one of the rewards of enlightened listening.

NOTATION

In order to appreciate the structure of Japanese music notation, one must first understand that traditional music is taught as a sonic, not a graphic, event. If notation is available it functions primarily as a memory aid for things previously learned aurally. This is quite evident in the vocal notation of the oldest genre of this study, the noh drama. Such notation developed out of earlier court and Buddhist chant systems.[18] The style of notation used in noh drama today is seen in our Sixth View (p. 198). The thicker neumes appearing along the right side of the column of text represent melodic conventions or ornaments, whereas the other characters indicate pitch areas or tempos.[19] Though the notation does provide considerable detail, there is much, particularly concerning rhythm, that can be performed only on the basis of experience or lessons.

The noh-flute notation is based on the ancient court tradition of using mnemonics that reflect melodic contour but do not denote specific pitches. The flute music for dance accompaniment consists primarily of four named, eight-beat melodic phrases (*kan*, *kan no chū*, *ryō*, and *ryō no chū*) plus conventional preludes or phrases that signal a section in the form.[20] Thus a memory-aid kind of notation is particularly appropriate. As published today, the mnemonics are set in columns on grids; the columns comprise eight squares, which represent eight beats.[21]

As mentioned in the Second View, the drum music of the noh can be found in a similar notation. Figure 13 is an excerpt from a score in which the flute and drum parts are shown together.[22] Counting columns from the right, the third column contains the ko tsuzumi part, the fourth contains the ō tsuzumi part, and the fifth shows the right and left strokes of the taiko plus the mnemonics of the flute. The same order is repeated in columns 7–9. The type of sound or stroke desired is indicated by the shape of the symbol used, and drum calls are shown, such as yo (written as ya because of its special pronunciation) in column 3 on the lines, between squares 3 and 4 and 11 and 12. The names of drum patterns can also be found, for example, *mitsuji* in column 3, square 11, and column 4, squares 6 and 14.

Figure 13 shows a Japanese example that comes closest to being a score in the Western sense. However, there is no conductor to use it, and the musicians themselves would never read parts derived from it. We shall soon learn that the time from beat to beat may not be even. Thus, for all its details it remains a reference to things learned aurally. There are similar scores that contain noh text and drum parts in columns.[23] However, they cannot be sight-read, because the actual rhythmic relationship between the drums and the voice is not shown. This seeming inadequacy is a reflection of the concept of relativity that is fundamental in this book. Accurate notation in the Western sense would be inaccurate in this music. One might even

45

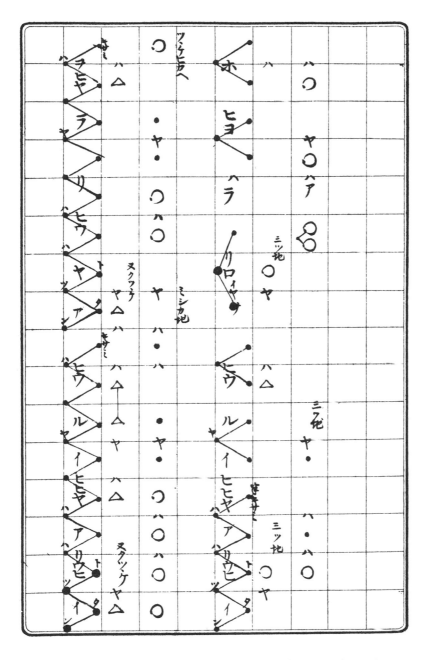

Figure 13. Noh hayashi notation. From the third page of the music for the dance *Jo no mai* in Morita Misao, ed., *Yōkyoku mai hyōshi taisei* (Osaka: Yoshida tokyoku shoten, 1914).

say that it would literally be "deadly" accurate, for it would kill the
flexibility of interpretation that underlies the flow of noh music in
actual performance. A more open-ended approach to notating the
drum music is found in books that consist of lists of the named, stereotyped patterns that are to be played during a given section of a
drama.[24] At first sight such notation might make the Western musician think of the figured bass of the baroque period or of the lead
sheet in popular music, but neither comparison is really accurate.
Both of the Western examples involve vertical sonorities (chords)
rather than linear time units (tetsuke). Both chords and time units
do have some flexibility in the timing of their appearance, and there
is an element of improvisation in the Western examples. However,
improvisation is absent from Japanese music, so one is left with the
questions, Where is the flexibility of noh music, and how does it
relate to the two forms of notation mentioned above? To answer these
questions one must look at the text, for both the vocal and the percussion lines are oriented to the words, particularly to the syllabic
structure of the poetry. The rules of performance are complicated and
in many cases hidden, but suffice to say that there are many passages
in which the singer may eliminate some of the half beats between
what appear to be eight evenly spaced beats in notation.[25] Thus notation becomes only a flexible framework rather than a representation
of the actual sonic event. The notated versions of passages show the
basic rhythm (*jibyōshi*), but that is not necessarily the performed
rhythm.[26] For example, in notation a vocal passage in the *hiranori*
rhythm and a so-called three-beat (mitsuji) style would be represented as follows:

$$8 . 1 . 2 . 3 . 4 . 5 . 6 . 7 . 8$$

In actual performance it may come out something like this:

$$8 . 12 . 34 . 56 . 7 . 8$$

How does a drummer coordinate an eight-beat pattern with this?
Sometimes he does not, for there are sections in which the singer and
the hayashi are rhythmically independent (fuai). However, when
they are rhythmically together (awase), the drummers obviously cannot be following notation. Awareness of the tradition and listening

to the syllabic style of the singer seem to be the secrets of the art, though I am not privy to such hidden knowledge and thus this statement must be accepted as conjecture. Apparently either the singer or the ō tsuzumi drummer may choose to perform a passage in some new style, in which case the other performers must adjust. Such differences in performance are quite radical by traditional Western standards, though not necessarily by the standards of the twentieth-century West. I hope this brief explanation of such differences will open the reader's mind, ears, and eyes to the fact that the Western notations of Japanese music such as are used in this book (as well as in previous studies) are convenient and necessary illusions, like still photographs of a flowing stream. Let us move on now to another tributary of Japan's theatrical music.

If we turn to the hayashi of shamisen music, we shall find both the grid and the lead-sheet notation of noh in use, for many of the same drum patterns appear in both noh and kabuki. There are, of course, other patterns that were created in the kabuki, but the addition of their names to the list does not affect the system of notation. However, the drums of shamisen music must sometimes be more directly integrated with the shamisen line. This style of drumming is called *chiri kara* after the mnemonic by which it is learned. It can be reduced to shorthand symbols that can easily be read *if* one already knows the shamisen line.[27]

The forms of hayashi notation mentioned above are used primarily for drumming in shamisen or dance (*buyō*) concerts or on the stage of the kabuki. The hayashi music of the offstage ensembles (geza) is usually found in a kabuki prompt book (tsukechō), which, as we noted in the Second View, merely tells one when to enter and what kind of thing to play.[28] The rest of the sonic information is in one's mind and ear and has been learned from a teacher who belongs to the guild involved in the performance. Guilds are an essential aspect of the system for, as we shall see, differences between guilds are musical as well as sociological.

Interest in notation for shamisen music has existed in Japan since the seventeenth century.[29] By now the reader should not be surprised to learn that the one early form that has remained viable today is the mnemonic system of "mouth shamisen" (*kuchi jamisen*). However, in

the past hundred years several different systems have been developed
in response to intrusions from the West. Since the shamisen is a melodic instrument, its music was readily susceptible to the fiction of
Western staff notation, but the most popular new forms were number notations somewhat like the French *chevé* system.[30] They had the
advantage of referring to finger positions or to a kind of movable-*do*
solfege and thus were able to allow the indigenous flexibility of
pitch that staff notation tends to inhibit. We noted above the rhythmic disjunction between the vocal line and the shamisen line. The
number notations along the text line are generally void of the rhythmic or metric implications of the shamisen part, and thus the singer
is better able to "read" the music with a proper rhythmic flow.[31]

It was mentioned earlier that, except for occasional hayashi part
books for noh dance, there are no scores as such.[32] The problem is
further compounded by the fact that the part books of one guild may
differ (and usually do differ) from those of another guild of performers on the same instruments. This lack of scores could be seen as a
way of protecting the secret knowledge of the music guilds. However, it may be more important as a system that forces performers to
have an overall sense of the music in order to play their own parts
successfully. Of course, musicians in other world traditions often
have the same sense of the music. However, in the genres under
study in this book the text is generally so important that the instrumentalists must maintain a great sensitivity to the vocal part. Perhaps the closest Western musical analogy is the relationship between
the pianist and singer in a fine lieder recital, though even in such
performances there is usually music with text on the piano rack.

The tsuzumi drummers in noh often must know the entire drama
by memory in order to play their parts. The shamisen players in the
gidayū genre of the puppet theater are famous for their ability, in
lessons, to sing and play by memory entire repertories. In the nagauta genre, instrumentalists demonstrate a similar knowledge of
the relation of their parts to the text.

By now it should be evident that both social and sonic relativity
are essential if one is to appreciate the nonimprovised but kaleido-
scopic traditions that we are discussing. Notation is obviously not an
area of primary concern in Japanese music. This being so, we must

turn to what is logically the next question: If notation is not the music, who is the composer and how does he work?

COMPOSITION

Despite the plethora of written materials in Japanese on the musical traditions discussed in this book, I have found the topic of the compositional process the most hidden. In our discussion of notation we found that secrets can be used to protect guild traditions or to assure artist control over the teaching and performance of given pieces. In the Prelude, we also noted that many secrets of Japanese music are not deliberately kept from the view of outsiders. Rather they may be hidden primarily because they are so deep within the traditions that no one thinks to write about them. The compositional process seems to fall into this category. Until more research is done in this area, I can only make some preliminary observations and hope that they may tempt better and/or younger scholars towards further exploration.

My impression is that traditional Japanese composition in noh and kabuki could be called communal. We know the names of noh playwrights and of the poets and "composers" of shamisen music. In shamisen music we often even know the date and place of the first performance as well as the name of the choreographer if the piece was used for dance accompaniment. However, the comments made earlier about rhythm, notation, and interpretation imply that the status of these original creators is not that of "the composer" in the Western sense. Perhaps it would be more appropriate to call such a creator the "first" composer. He has provided a framework that allows for continual creativity in future performances.[33] I am not referring to improvisation, variation, or the reordering of the sections of a piece. Rather, *interpretation* and *orchestration* seem to be the Western terms that best apply. They can be more easily applied in traditional Japanese music because the original compositional process is generally not concerned with highly personal originality. The skillful manipulation of sonic conventions of a Japanese music genre reminds us of similar artistry in much traditional East Asian ink painting. There one sees the same mountains, flowers, boats, or creatures and is captivated by the consummate skill with which the artist draws the same image again; it is exactly correct and may be different from earlier versions, but it is not the difference that makes it art. In the noh drama, much of the music seems as rigid and transparent as much Western classical music. However, the actor may choose to re-interpret a passage, so that the drummers will have to change totally the pattern that they play. The tsuzumi drummer, as noted earlier, may also instigate changes.

My limited experience with noh music does not allow me to pursue the subject of its creative process any further. Instead, let me speak of nagauta. Though I have never been present when a new piece was written, I can offer some impressions based on twenty-five years of studying the nagauta repertory.

It would appear that a shamisenist, a singer, or both will commission or borrow a text and set it according to their tastes or, if it is a theater piece, to the needs of a dancer or actor. The percussion and flute parts are then added under the direction of the head (*hayashi gashira*) of the percussion ensemble that is to perform the piece. The name of this contributor is seldom listed with the name(s) of the original composer(s), so, in Western terms, one might be tempted to call him an arranger. However, our analysis will show that the integration of the drum and flute parts often displays an awareness of textual and structural needs that is beyond that associated with mere orchestration. I regard the "arranger" as a co-composer in a communal creative effort.

Once the original cooperative effort has been made, a nagauta composition is still not necessarily complete. As long as the original composers are performing the piece, it will tend to remain as unchanged as a comparable piece in the Western classical tradition. However, we have pointed out in other contexts how important are the differences between guilds of performers. The differences in another guild's performance of the shamisen part are generally rather subtle, whereas the singers within one group have considerable opportunities for different rhythmic and even melodic interpretations. The music of the basic hayashi is also subject to only slight guild-identifying differences, but there is room for new orchestrations if new tone colors will enhance the atmosphere or meaning of the text.

If the piece is a dance accompaniment, more radical changes or additions may be made to suit the needs of a new choreographer. In the Japanese view, all these renditions are the same piece. This is equally true whether the work is performed by only one singer and a shamisen in a concert hall or by a full ensemble in a kabuki theater.

Given all the potential variables mentioned above, it should be evident that the creative process in nagauta does not end with a composition's first performance. To a certain extent Western music has enjoyed some of this creativity in its own concert halls. New instruments like the piano and modern violin, and new approaches to dynamics and tempi, have allowed us to display musical museum pieces in new colors, while some ensembles concentrate on attempting to reveal the original sounds of these pieces through "authentic" performance. Japan seems to give its living musicians their creative outlet through the ongoing communal compositional process.

Another important caveat regarding Western use of notation in the study of such music is in order here. One must not regard the notation or transcription of a composition as "the piece." Rather, see it as one version of a communal composition that, if performed again by the same musicians, will probably come out precisely the same, but may be quite different if musicians from other guilds play it. The concept of relativity is once more most useful in appreciating Japanese music. Though a given piece is "set," it will not look or sound the same if experienced from the perspectives of different musicians in other performances. Historically these differences may have reflected the need for hidden guild traditions. However, in modern times they may be auspicious signs that concerts of "old" music are not museums filled with rigid fossils, but rather are presentations of living, ongoing traditions. It is with this view that we enter into our analytical studies.

Shakkyō, a Bridge between Noh and Kabuki Music—One Story in Two Genres

In our first two views of Japanese music, we looked at the making of a drum and then at the process by which one learns to play drums. Our next step is to look at music in which drums are important. The major sources for such music are the noh and kabuki dramas and the compositions that developed out of them for separate music or dance concerts. The piece *Shakkyō*, "The Stone Bridge," and variants on it provide examples of all these categories, and are well known in Japan. Thus, *Shakkyō* has been chosen as the basis of our first comparative study. Since the drums are used in both vocal and purely instrumental sections, we shall refer to melodic as well as percussion lines in our comparisons. With such topics and famous compositions our view should become wider as we circumambulate the base of Japan's beautiful mount of music.

The last image is particularly apt, for the stone bridge of this story is literally found at a "cool, refreshing mountain" (*seiryō-san*), though the geographical setting is China. The roots of the story may also be found in China, but the earliest Japanese version is said to be in the *Jikkin-shō*, a three-volume collection of moral tales credited to Rokuhara Jirōzaemon (ca. 1252).[1] However, it is the noh version and its kabuki and concert adaptations for which we have known musical accompaniments, so we shall limit ourselves to these versions of the story.

Ōe no Sadamoto (961–1034),[2] a nobleman who became a priest, is on a pilgrimage to India and China. At Ch'ing Liang Mountain[3] in China he comes upon an unusual natural bridge. Before he is able to cross it, he is stopped by a woodcutter (an old man or a boy) who explains that even the holiest of priests have found crossing this bridge very difficult. The magic nature and dangers of the bridge are described. The woodcutter then explains that the Bodhisattva Man-jusri lives among the flowers and music on the other side of the bridge and that, if the priest will wait, the Bodhisattva will appear. After the woodcutter leaves in an actual production of the noh play, a white-peony tree and red-peony tree are placed on the two sides of a small dais in the center of the stage. A lion then appears and dances vigorously among the flowers, thus ending the play. In some productions two lions appear, and each school of noh has a slightly different version of both the text and the choreography.

Though this play has been in constant use for centuries, it has seldom been studied by foreign scholars. This is due primarily to a prejudice against its text. Though it is heavily endowed with Bud-dhist images and dramatic pictorialisms, the text has not proved to be challenging to Western scholars of Japanese literature or theology. What has kept *Shakkyō* alive in Japan is its choreography and its music. The literary conventions and thin plot line come to life on a stage. Thus, the version of the text that we shall present here should be regarded not as a literary work but rather as one of the media through which we might be able to discover some of the power of the theatrical event.

Scholars are not sure who was the author of the first noh version of *Shakkyō*, though it is often credited to Jūrō Motomasa (1395–

1459).[4] However, at least one lion dance was part of the repertory of Zeami Motokiyo (1363–1444), one of the founders of noh, and lion dances were part of earlier theatrical forms,[5] so any claim of first use is relative. All lion-dance plays in noh drama are presently categorized as *Shakkyō* plays to distinguish them from the variety of lion dances that have been used in folk festivals.[6]

The rising popular kabuki theater of the seventeenth century was quick to recognize the value of both lion-dance traditions. Their popularity and variety are evident in Figure 14, a partial list of kabuki lion dances. Figures 15 and 16 illustrate the continuity of the tradition over some three centuries of kabuki.[7] The eighteenth- and early-nineteenth-century drawings in Figure 15 contain many of the kabuki innovations in the lion-dance tradition. First note that many of these early *Shakkyō*-based dances were performed by female impersonators (*onnagata*; see Figure 15a). This had an important influence on their texts, which began to refer more to customs and locations in the brothel areas of Japan than to those of the sacred mountains of China. Such textural changes allowed for considerable choreographic and musical interplay between the lion-dance styles of street festivals and those derived from *Shakkyō*.[8]

Shakkyō-based lion dances	Festival-derived lion dances
Aioijishi (1734)	*Kuruwajishi* (1777, kiyomoto)
Shakkyō (1738) (*Tsukaijishi*)	*Echigojishi* (1811)
Hanabusa shishi no rangyōku (1742), later called *Makurajishi*	*Kakubeijishi* (1828, nagauta and tokiwazu)
Hanabusa shūjaku no shishi (1754)	*Ikajishi* (1834)
Futari shakkyō (1768)	*Kagamejishi* (1893)
Shakkyō (1820)	*Azumajishi* (1907, tokiwazu)
Yuki no shakkyō or *Shakkyō no setsukei* (1839)	
Renjishi (1861)	
Mochizuki (1870)	
Shin-shakkyō (1878)	

Figure 14. Selected kabuki lion dances.

Despite the great variety of plots and styles in the kabuki versions of *Shakkyō*, the last lines of the original noh text (lines 87–99 in the following translation) tend to be used for all the finales. However, truncated versions of the instrumental interlude (*raijo*) and the exciting hayashi-accompanied dance (*ranjo*) are common. Two kabuki choreographic additions have become conventional as well. One is the use of a very long lion's mane, which is flung in circles as the result of quick head movements. The other is the presence of butterflies (Figure 15a) with which the lion cavorts in pseudoferocious chases.[9] Under the influence of the folk forms, the kabuki lion is sometimes reduced to a head on the dancer's hand that quite frightens the dancer as much as the butterflies. There are even lion heads that are symbolized by two open fans used as snapping jaws. They may appear as a headdress or be held in the hand, and there can be two fans in each hand. Many of the features mentioned above are seen in Figure 15. The number of lions also varies (see Figure 15b). We mentioned that one or two lions may be used on the noh stage. In kabuki the number can increase to three, though one or two is more common. However, readers who are former students of mine will recall my favorite aphorism, "Stay loose," and be prepared for a host of lions in some of the gaudier productions. We can see in Figure 16 that the bridge itself is often added to modern kabuki productions. Despite all these possible changes, the basic features of the lion and the peonies of the original noh drama *Shakkyō* remain consistent both in the kabuki text and on its stage.

The kabuki lion dances obviously reduced the influence of the original noh drama to a minimum. However, in the nineteenth century the growth of concert (*ozashiki*) shamisen music (particularly in the nagauta genre) and the maturation of kabuki itself led to a greater interest in noh drama as a source of new compositional inspiration.[10] In 1820 Kineya Saburōsuke IV (1800–1859) composed a nagauta concert piece called *Shakkyō*.[11] The composition is also known as *Geki-bushi shakkyō* because Kineya based his work not only on the original noh text but also on an old tradition of narrative shamisen music known as *geki-bushi*.[12] This genre of shamisen music is related historically to another earlier shamisen genre called *ōzatsuma-bushi*.

The obvious first question is, Why did Kineya rely on a different shamisen genre for a new kind of nagauta music on a noh text? The answer is that geki and ōzatsuma relied heavily on a set of named, stereotyped shamisen patterns[13] that were created to support dialogues in a recitative manner. Such options were not normally avail-

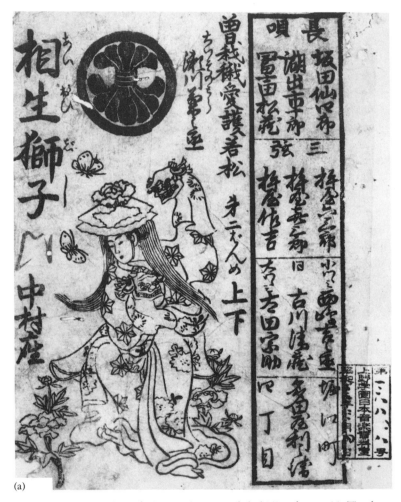

(a)

Figure 15. Eighteenth- and nineteenth-century kabuki lion dances. (a) The dance piece *Aioijishi* of 1734. Courtesy of the Japanese Music Research Archive, Ueno Gakuen. (b) The dance piece *Yuki no shakkyō* of 1839. Courtesy of the Tsubouchi Memorial Theatre Museum, Waseda University.

able to nagauta composers as theirs was basically a lyrical tradition. Throughout the nineteenth and early twentieth centuries nagauta composers found such ōzatsuma patterns most useful in setting narrative lines previously delivered by actors or narrators while maintaining their lyrical style for other sections of the piece. Thus,

(b)

Kineya was able to approach the challenge of a "serious" nagauta concert composition based on noh with a battery of stylistic options. In the process, he has provided us with an excellent topic for comparative musicological study. Let us begin with the text.

Some claim that Kineya took his text directly from that of the noh.[14] So far no published noh text has been found that coincides precisely with that of the nagauta composition.[15] Since this study is primarily musical, any references to the noh text will be based on the version found in the Kanze school recording from which noh musical examples have been drawn. This version is 41 lines longer than the text of the nagauta piece and is organized in conventional formal units of the noh drama. If the names of noh formal units do not appear in the nagauta text as well, they are given in parentheses in our translation (e.g., *nanori* before line 1). The names of noh or nagauta formal units that appear in the nagauta text are not in parentheses (e.g., *utai-gakari*). In a nagauta performance the use of solo or group singing varies, but to capture the style of the original piece indica-

Figure 16. A twentieth-century kabuki lion dance by Onoe Baiko. Photo courtesy of Yoshida Chiaki.

tion is made of which sections are performed in noh by the main actor (shite), the supporting actor (waki), or the chorus (ji). Phrases or lines that do not appear in the Kanze noh recording are underlined. It is not germane to the purpose of this study to indicate as well which noh lines are missing from the nagauta version or to indicate the manner in which a few lines appear in a different order or placement. Moreover, explanations of the literary references in the text have been limited to comments found in the footnotes to the translation. The first function of the text is to help the reader capture some of the spirit of the play. It will also serve as a convenient reference point when we begin to study the musical similarities and differences of one story in two Japanese traditions.

SHAKKYŌ

Utai-gakari (*Nanori*)
Waki

1. Kore wa Ōe no Sadamoto
   shukke shi

2. Jakushō Hōshi nite sōrō
3. ware nittō toten no nozomi
   sōraite hatō o koe
4. kore wa haya Shakkyō nite
   sōrō
5. mukai wa Monju no jōdo
   Seiryō-san nite sōrō hodo
   ni
6. kono atari ni yasurai
7. hashi o watarabaya to omoi
   sōrō

I am the dharma master Jakushō,
   who left home as Ōe no
   Sadamoto.
With the hope of entering China
and crossing to India, I have
   passed over the billowy waves,
and have now arrived at Stone
   Bridge.
Mount Qingliang[16] of Manjusri's
   Pure Land is on the other side,

I think that I shall cross over
this bridge after I rest here awhile.

(*Issei*)
Shite

8. Matsukaze no
9. hana o takigi ni fukisoete

10. yuki o mo hakobu yamaji
    kana

A pinewind blows
against my firewood, frosting it
   with cherry blossoms:
oh, the mountain path, where I
   even carry snow.

Aikata

11. shōka bokuteki no ko

Sounds of a woodcutter's song and a
   herdboy's flute.[17]

12. ningen banji samazama ni — The karma of humans is to pass through a world
13. yo o watariyuku waza nagara — in one of myriad ways.

(*Sageuta*)

14. amari ni yama o tōku kite — Having come quite far through the mountains,
15. kumo mata ato o tachihedate — where clouds have formed and veiled my footprints,

(*Ageuta*)

16. iritsuru kata mo shiranami no — I do not even know the way I have come,
17. tani no kawaoto ame to nomi — only as rain do I hear the river sounds in the valley of white waves,
18. kikoete matsu no kaze mo nashi — and I hear no longer the wind in the pines.
19. Ge ni ayamatte — Truly I have been lost.
20. hanjitsu no kaku tarishi mo — for though I have been a guest for half a day
21. ima mi no ue ni shiraretsutsu — now I myself know the true time.[18]
22. Tsumagi seoute ono katage — Carrying brushwood on my back and shouldering an ax,
23. iwane hageshiki sobazutai — I go along a precipitous place where the crags below are severe,
24. ozasa o wakete ayumi kuru — and come sauntering, parting the young bamboo grasses.

Mondō
Waki

25. Ika ni sore naru yamabito — Hello there, mountain dweller,
26. kore wa Shakkyō nite sōrō ka — is this Stone Bridge?

Shite

27. San zōrō — It is so,
28. kore wa Shakkyō nite sōrō yo — this is indeed Stone Bridge.
29. mukai wa Monju no jōdo nite — On the other side is the Pure Land of Manjusri,[19]
30. Seiryō-san to zo mōsu nari — and it is called Mount Qingliang,
31. yokuyoku on-ogami sorae — so you would do well to pay your respects.

Waki

32. <u>Waga mi no ue</u> o butsu<u>ryo</u> ni makase

Entrusting my life to the Buddha's expectations,

33. hashi o watarabaya to omoi sōrō

I would like to cross over the bridge.

Shite

34. Shibaraku sōrō

Wait a minute!

35. sono kami <u>nari</u>

In days long past,

36. na o etamaishi kōsō

even renowned high priests,

37. <u>kisō to kikoeshi hito mo</u>

and even people known as venerable priests,

38. koko nite tsukihi o okuri <u>tamai</u>

have spent days and months here,

39. nangyō kugyō shashin no gyō nite <u>koso</u>

with acts of austerity, penance, and relinquishing the body.

40. hashi o mo watari tamaishi <u>ga</u>

Only then did they ever cross the bridge.

41. shishi wa <u>kochū</u> o <u>haman</u> tote mo

But, as they say, even if a lion eats a small insect,[20]

42. mazu ikioi o nasu to koso kike

he first prepares himself to do so!

43. waga hōriki no areba tote

If you were to have dharma powers,

44. tayasuku omoi wataran <u>koto</u>

you probably would think it easy to cross [the bridge of stone],

45. ara ayōshi no on-koto ya

but what a precarious act it would be!

Waki

46. Iware o kikeba arigata ya

Now that I've heard the story, it is really extraordinary;

47. naonao <u>kono</u> hashi no iware <u>kuwashiku</u> on-monogatari sōrae <u>ya</u>

but do tell me more particulars about the history of the bridge.

Shite

48. <u>katatte kikase mōsubeshi</u>

I shall tell you the story.

(*Kuri*)
Ji

49. Sore tenchi kaikyaku no kono kata

The bridge has been here since the first parting of heaven and earth.

50. uro o kudashite kokudo o wataru

Coming down through the rain and dew, it crosses the country,

51. kore sunawachi ama no ukihashi tomo ieri

and thus is also called the floating bridge of heaven.[21]

(*Sashi*)
Shite

52. sono hoka kokudo sekai ni oite

Elsewhere in the country and the world

53. hashi no nadokoro samazama ni shite

there are all sorts of famous bridge sites.

Ji

54. suiha no nan o nogarete wa

It may indeed be due to the goodness of bridges

55. banmin tomeri yo o wataru mo

that myriad people are able to escape from drowning in water and wave

56. sunawachi hashi no toku to ka ya

and pass safely across the bountiful world.

(*Kuse*)

57. Shikaru ni kono shakkyō wa
58. iwao gagataru ganseki ni
59. onore to kakaru hashi nareba

However, because this stone bridge is a bridge that hangs by itself on crags and rock, jagged and towering high,

60. Shakkyō to koso nazuketare
61. ge ni kono hashi no arisama wa

it has been named Stone Bridge. The conditions on the bridge

62. sono omote wazuka ni shite
63. shaku yori wa semau

are truly severe: its surface is small, narrower than a foot;

64. wataseru nagasa sanjō amari

it spans a distance of more than thirty feet;

65. koke wa namerite ashi mo tamarazu

the moss upon it is slippery so that one's feet will not rest firm;

66. tani no sokubaku fukaki koto su senjō to mo oboetari

and the abyss of the canyon seems to be more than ten thousand feet.

Shite

67. haruka ni mine o miagureba

When the peaks are viewed from a distance

Ji

68. kumo yori otsuru aradaki ni

the mists are murky and dark

Ai

69. kiri mōrō to kurau shite	around the wild waterfall falling from the clouds.
70. shita wa nairi mo shiranami no	With sounds of white waves reverberating in the tempest
71. oto wa arashi ni hibiki aite	it seems to be hell down below.
72. kokū o wataru ga gotoku nari	It is like crossing an empty space.
73. hashi no keshiki o miwataseba	On looking over the scene of the bridge,
74. kumo ni sobiyuru yosōi wa	its array, which soars into the clouds,
75. tatowaba sekiyō no ame no nochi	is like the form a rainbow takes
76. niji o naseru sono katachi mata	after a rain at eventide,
77. yumi o hikeru gotoku nite	or the shape of a drawn bow.
78. jinpen butsuriki ni arazu shite wa	Without the permutations of a god or the powers of a Buddha,
79. susunde hito ya wataru beki	who will advance and cross over?
80. mukai wa Monju no jōdo nite	On the other side is the Pure Land of Manjusri,
81. tsune ni seiga no hana furite	where flowers continually fall to the accompaniment of pipes and songs;
82. shō jaku kin kugo	mouth organs, zithers, and harps
83. yūhi no kumo ni kikoyu beki	may be heard from beyond the clouds around the evening sun.
84. mokuzen no kidoku arata nari	It is an auspicious miracle before our eyes.
85. shibaraku matase tamae ya	Wait awhile!
86. yogo no jisetsu mo ima iku hodo ni yo mo sugiji	Before long the time will come for a heavenly apparition [of Manjusri].

Raijo (Raijo)
Ranjo (Ranjo)
Kurui Ai no Te (Shishi Mai)
Chirashi (Kiri)
Ji

87. Shishi Toraden no bugaku no migin	The season for the Shishi and Toraden music and dance.[22]
88. shishi Toraden no bugaku no migin	The season for the Shishi and Toraden music and dance.

89. botan no hanabusa nioi michi michi	Peony blooms: full, full with fragrance!
90. taikin rikin no shishigashira	The lion's head with great muscular strength—
91. ute ya hayase ya	prancing and playing,
92. botanbō botanbō	peony perfume, peony perfume,
93. kōkin no zui arawarete	the stamens of golden yellow, coming forth,
94. hana ni tawamure eda ni fushi marobi	frolic in the flowers, lie down and roll in the branches.
95. ge ni mo ue naki shishi ō no ikioi	The authority of the Lion King, truly unsurpassed:
96. nabikanu kusaki mo naki toki nare ya	indeed it is a time when all the plants and trees bow to it!
97. banzei senshu to maiosame	For myriad harvests and a thousand autumns, he perfects his dance,
98. banzei senshu to maiosame	for myriad harvests and a thousand autumns, he perfects his dance,

Dangire

99. shishi no za ni koso naorikere	and he seats himself on the Lion Throne![23]

Having surveyed the history, plot line, and text of *Shakkyō*, we can now turn to its music. Ideally, the reader should experience a complete recording (or better yet a complete performance) of the nagauta and noh versions before entering into this study. We have been able to provide a few samplings of the sounds so that the reader will not take the primitive information of examples in Western notation as a true representation of the wonders of the original musical events. Let us now start on our comparative music path to the Stone Bridge and the sight of a lion.

THE NANORI, ISSEI, AND AGEUTA

Before the text begins, there is in both the noh and the nagauta version a solo noh-flute introduction, the *nanoribue* or *nanori fue*. The noh version is longer as its function is to accompany the slow entrance of the waki actor along the passageway (*hashigakari*) between the exit curtain and the stage. The actor traditionally stops at the first pillar of the stage, where characters identify themselves (the *nanori*). Such a long selection is not necessary in the nagauta version as this piece was designed for concert use and thus no actor enters at all. Differences in the actual melodies of the flutes can be attributed to this truncation and to the fact that the flutists belong to different guilds.[24]

Example 3* is an attempt to capture some of the differences in the opening vocal passage. Example 3a represents this passage as sung on the noh recording, 3b this passage as sung by Kineya Roku-zaemon on a nagauta recording, and 3c this passage as sung by Yoshi-zumi Ijurō on another nagauta recording.[25] As noted in the Inter-lude, the basic pitch of a nagauta piece is set by the singer and may vary from performance to performance. Thus, central pitch differ-ences in Example 3 do not affect the comparison. Unfortunately, it is not possible to evoke the differences in vocal quality in notation. Suf-fice to say that all three performers sing rather back in the throat

Example 3. Three versions of the opening passage of *Shakkyō* (cassette example A).

with loose jowls and slow, wide vibratos. The nagauta singers push the tone more forward, and, in Western terms, one might say that Yoshizumi has more of a tenor's quality and Rokuzaemon more of a baritone's. What is evident from Example 3 is the more dramatic nature of kabuki imitations of noh singing. The differences in tempo and contour shown here are typical of later noh imitations not only in this piece but in the nagauta repertory in general. Stylistic differences in enunciation can be noted by listening to the recordings. In sum, it is evident from this first passage that we are dealing with two similar yet very different traditions.

The *issei* section of the noh drama opens with an instrumental interlude played by the flute and the ō and ko tsuzumi drums for the entrance of the shite actor. Example 4a* shows the opening phrase of the vocal line that follows, as sung by the shite on the recording. Example 4b* is a transcription of the same passage as notated in the nagauta score.[26] In the noh version one finds a rather typical accompaniment by the ō and ko tsuzumi. Through the use of named, stereotyped patterns (listed at the end of Example 4a), the drums are able to hold the vocal line in a general eight-beat frame that is set in a flexible rather than metronomic beat. The nagauta version of this section begins without any instrumental introduction except for that given by the shamisen in the first four measures. At this point, we obviously have moved into a musical tradition totally different from that of the original noh. At the end of text line 10, however, the noh flute enters in the nagauta version in a style similar to that of the opening of the issei played earlier in the noh version. This is followed by an instrumental interlude for shamisen and hayashi (i.e., the two tsuzumi and the noh flute). The placement of the instrumental interlude at this point in the nagauta piece is a logical adjustment to the conventions of kabuki dance form (see p. 37). An experienced listener will have felt the opening section through line 10 as the oki of the form, and is thus prepared to hear an instrumental michiyuki, a section that in kabuki music would signal the entrance of an actor or dancer. The nagauta composition maintains some of the flavor of the original noh by using noh-style drum patterns behind the shamisen melody. Example 5* shows an excerpt from this

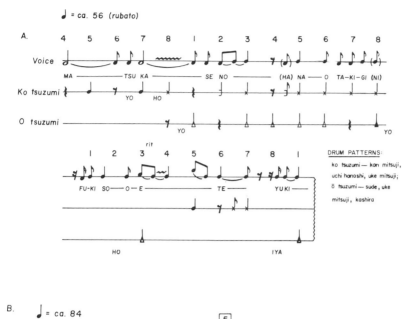

Example 4. A noh and a nagauta version of the issei opening in *Shakkyō* (cassette example B).

Example 5. An excerpt from the michiyuki section of the nagauta *Shakkyō* (cassette example C).

interlude in which the shamisen line in fact seems to adjust to the rhythm of the drum pattern that one might have originally thought of as a mere underpinning for the melodic line. Compare, for example, the *uchi hanashi* pattern in Example 4a (with its added beat) and the similar pattern in Example 5. (Pattern names are shown in parentheses in Example 5.) This mixture of noh drum patterns with long notes on the noh flute serves to give a proper noh flavor while the shamisen and singer proceed in normal kabuki style. By line 14, when the *sageuta* of the noh appears, one finds the nagauta piece using only voice and shamisen in a freer rhythmic style that implies a cadence.

In the noh recording, the *ageuta* section (line 16) is accompanied by the ō and ko tsuzumi plus interjections by the flute. All the imagery of lines 17 and 18 seems to have no effect on the noh melody, though the music does slow down as it approaches the cadence at the end of line 18. The nagauta version of these lines attempts to produce some of the rhythmic flexibility of noh while remaining in the more "modern" nagauta tradition. The word *kikoete* in line 18 is accompanied by a standard shamisen pattern called *jo* from the geki-ōzatsuma tradition, the tradition that gave this piece its extra title. Recall that the composer had deliberately wanted to prove how such recitative patterns could be used successfully to handle noh text.

Example 6* shows that the composer had no intention of merely writing a parlando composition. Here is obvious word painting of the pine branches (*matsu*) waving in a wind that the woodcutter no longer hears. The example is transcribed from the shamisen notation. Cassette example D demonstrates how relative the vocal line is

Example 6. Word painting in the printed vocal line of the nagauta *Shakkyō* (cassette example D of a recorded version).

Example 7. Word painting in the printed shamisen line of the nagauta *Shakkyō* (cassette example E of a recorded version).

to the interpretation of a particular singer. Example 7* shows yet another musical reaction to the text, for the shamisen clearly totters along the precipitous crags (line 23). It is the balance between the demands of parlando imitations of noh and shamisen interests in word painting that makes the study of the composition of this piece particularly rewarding.

THE MONDŌ, KURI, SASHI, AND KUSE

As can be heard in cassette example F, the *mondō* of a noh drama
consists mostly of dialogue. Thus it should not be surprising that
the nagauta composer made extensive use of ōzatsuma patterns in
setting the same text. Example 8a* shows the nagauta setting of
lines 25–26. As the voice part is entirely declamatory, only its text
is shown along with the shamisen accompaniment. The terms in parentheses are the names of ōzatsuma patterns from which the shamisen part is derived. The sparse, disjunct style of the shamisen part is
characteristic of ōzatsuma patterns, as is the tendency to emphasize
the pitch centers F-sharp and B, along with the whole-step upper
leading tone, C-sharp. Example 8b shows that, even in short vocal

Example 8. Ōzatsuma patterns in the mondō of the nagauta *Shakkyō* (cassette example F of noh mondō excerpt and of 8a).

exclamations (*serifu*) in a basically lyrical line, the ōzatsuma-preferred tonalities will appear for that brief moment (m. 8, line 54).

The ōzatsuma style is maintained throughout the mondō (to line 48) and continues for the first line of the *kuri*, even though in the noh the first line would be sung by the chorus (the ji). The transition to a new setting occurs in line 51, as shown in Example 9*. The tsuzumi enter in noh patterns, and the noh flute is also heard, while

Example 9. An excerpt from the kuri section of the nagauta *Shakkyō* (cassette example G).

the beat becomes more metronomic. The brief shamisen interlude that follows is accompanied by drums that, for the first time in the piece, play in kabuki style. As the story unfolds and the pace quickens, the music in general moves closer to kabuki traditions and further from those of the noh. Perhaps the composer, having proved that the piece originated in noh, feels more at home in the tradition in which he was trained.

The section known as a *sashi* in the noh (lines 52−56) is in this kabuki style in the nagauta piece. The nagauta interest in text setting that we noted earlier continues in what would be the *kuse* section in the noh (lines 57−86). Example 10 illustrates a most interesting musical convention used in nagauta for dramatic effects, namely, the sudden use of A as a pitch center and nuclear tone for a miyako tetrachord with the resulting B-flat half-step upper leading tone. As shown in Example 10a, the kuse opens with a tonally ambiguous phrase. Do we have a half cadence in measure 8 or have we modulated? The answer comes in the next passage with a miyako tetrachord on A, plus minyō and miyako tetrachords on its fifth, E. All this happens when the jagged crags and rocks (*gagataru ganseki*) are mentioned. By the time we turn in the text to the bridge that hangs by itself (*onore to kakaru*), we have returned to an F-sharp and B tonal area (mm. 15−17).

Example 10b is a transcription of the shamisen setting of lines 64−65, in which the thirty-foot bridge is described as slippery with moss. The B-flat is combined with a jerking rhythm (mm. 8−9) when the foot can find no stand (*ashi mo tamarazu*), and even the shamisen slips (m. 11), to bring the phrase to a cadence on E. The next B-flat in the piece occurs in the setting of line 72, shown in Example 10c. It occurs on the word for empty space (*kokū*) and indeed creates a most ambiguous sense of tonality.

The only other use of the pitch B-flat with text in the entire composition is shown in Example 10d, a transcription of the shamisen accompaniment of line 86 in the finale.[27] The meaning of this B-flat in relation to the text is not obvious, since it occurs on the term for court dancing (*bugaku*), and this word is treated differently in the setting of the next line. Perhaps the use of B-flat here is more a matter of general dramatic effect, for the tempo and melody have just changed in order to build towards an exciting ending. Whatever the specific reason may be for the use of B-flat in this passage, a study of the four examples of its use in the overall composition seems to reinforce the idea that this particular tonal area is saved for special effects in nagauta.[28]

Not all text setting is accomplished solely by the shamisen line. Example 11 begins with an interlude that occurs right after line 67, when one is looking upward (*miagureba*) while in a deep valley. The call-response style of the shamisen and drums recalls a kabuki drum convention called echo (*kodama*) that is commonly used when a scene is set in the mountains.[29] The composer telescopes the shamisen version of the echo motive in measures 6–7 before moving on to the next passage. There is a still subtler signal of this nature earlier in

Example 10. Shamisen modulations in the nagauta *Shakkyō*.

Example 11. Mood setting in the shamisen music of the nagauta *Shakkyō*.

line 66, for the word *tani* (valley) is accompanied by the same two pitches that begin Example 11, played in a similar rhythm. Such an adumbration of the use of a convention in a later interlude is strong evidence of the concern of nagauta composers for proper text setting.

As the music moves on to the next line in Example 11, the rhythmic density of the shamisen part is intensified by the direct support of kabuki-style drumming. The use of double stops in measure 14 (and in the next twelve measures) is yet another standard kabuki manner of creating an exciting, dense musical texture for a dramatic moment.

THE RAIJO AND RANJO

In the noh drama, just before these sections there is often a *kyōgen* interlude. Since such a section is purely narrative and its text is not included in *Shakkyō*, we need not consider it in this study. Raijo, however, is a different matter. In noh drama, raijo (the term means "coming-out introduction") is a short hayashi pattern that can be used to signify the end of one section and thus the start of another.[30]

It is not used by all schools of noh in the performance of *Shakkyō*.[31] Its function as a transitional section is reflected in the nagauta *Shakkyō*, for there is a shamisen interlude called raijo that is to be played only if there are no drums available for the concert.[32] Since the recordings used for this study employ full ensembles, we shall concentrate on the shamisen hayashi rendition. In this and the next section of our kabuki version of a noh play we can see most clearly how the earlier tradition was transported into the later. Cassette examples H–J present the types of *raijo* and *ranjo* discussed below.

The term *ranjo* means "agitated introduction," and any experience of its sounds will reinforce the logic of its name. It is one of the most powerful and "contemporary"-sounding interludes in all hayashi music. It is also unique in that the first half of the interlude is performed without dancers or singers. A rare example of purely instrumental music in noh, it is easily transformed into kabuki or concert versions of the same play. It is one of the few examples of noh hayashi music that is played in kabuki and nagauta concerts without the addition of other instrumental parts or significant changes in the original hayashi music. Therefore, we are able to study both noh and kabuki music in one place as we enter the sounds and structure of ranjo.

In the context of the original noh drama, ranjo seems to be divided into two sections. The first is sometimes called the dew (*tsuyu*) interlude, in which sounds of the deep mountain valley set the scene. The second section is meant for the entrance (*tōjō*) of the lion onto the passageway that leads to the main stage.[33] The music of ranjo and, to some extent, that of the lion dance that follows are considered secret pieces (hikyoku), and there is a limited amount of notation of them to this day. If one listens to the attenuated flute line and tense tsuzumi-taiko dialogue with which ranjo begins, one will realize that such elastic passages would not be easily represented in notation in any case. Example 12a* shows the way in which the opening (*raijo*) pattern is notated in the nagauta hayashi tradition with the drum calls romanized. To turn this notation into a performance, one has to feel as though one were a large rubber band that stretches with great tension and then suddenly snaps. Since there is

no improvisation in this music, the "proper" performance of all of
ranjo remains one of the greatest challenges in Japanese drum playing. Example 12b* shows all the notation that exists for its first section. In the noh drama this section might be regarded as a moment
of truth for both the taiko and the ko tsuzumi player. The eight-beat
pattern is played three times, but the last two taiko strokes should

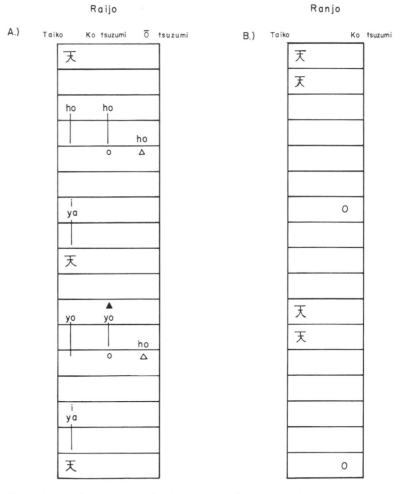

Example 12. Drum notation for the patterns raijo and ranjo (patterns in cassette
examples H–J).

be stronger in the third statement and should be played with space (ma) between them (cassette examples J and Kc). The most terrifying moment for the ko tsuzumi player is the performance of the single pon indicated by the circle in Example 12b. Its sound must be absolutely correct, and the space between it and the taiko sound can be felt only through deep breathing and, once more, a sense of ma.[34]

In some schools of noh and most often in nagauta renditions of ranjo the two taiko strokes are answered by two ta on the ko tsuzumi (cassette examples H, I, or Ka, Kb). This may relate to a mountain-echo (kodama) effect.[35] However, such direct calls and responses have less magic than the single, open sound and deliberate suppression of the sense of a beat (compare cassette examples I and J or cassette examples Kb and Kc). In some nagauta hayashi performances another dramatic effect is achieved by filling the time between the taiko stroke and a ko tsuzumi ta with the creaking sound of slowly tightening ropes. I obviously find the silence more powerful.

Listening to the ranjo excerpts on the book cassette, one notes that whereas some nagauta musicians are able to maintain the sense of tension, others tend to play this passage rather mechanically. This may be due to the fact that these recordings were made for dancers' use. Since no dancing occurs in this section, there may have been pressure on the drummers not to linger on their solos so that the music can return to being dance accompaniment. Another factor may have been the amount of space available on the record bands. In any case, the performance of ranjo, or the aural experience of it, remains one of the most unusual sonic events in traditional Japanese music.

The last section of ranjo (deru no ranjo) accompanies the slow, menacing entrance of the lion. Though the beat remains quite elastic, the texture becomes more dense and dramatic. There are solo taiko passages that sound particularly improvisatory, but by now the reader should not be surprised to learn that they are quite specific. A study of a taiko lesson book[36] or a viewing of the actual noh play will reveal that the drum patterns relate directly to the lion's movements. The section ends with the full hayashi in a crescendo and accelerando accompaniment as the lion moves onto the main stage and begins its dance.

THE KURUI AI NO TE (SHISHI MAI)

The lion dance (*shishi mai*) is the high point of *Shakkyō*. Musically it is particularly useful to us because it contains the major instrumental section and thus is easier to study using Western conventions of notation. To reveal the "hidden" views of this music we shall speak first of its form as described in noh theory and then compare the performance practices of noh and kabuki.

In noh, dances are divided into sections (*dan*), the lengths of which are usually measured in terms of the number of eight-beat patterns (yatsubyōshi) played by the flute and the drums. Since the taiko is normally used only in dance sections and dance music is often discussed in terms of the role of the flute, we shall limit our study to these two members of the hayashi. A *shishi mai* is heard in cassette example K.

The noh lion dance varies in length from six to twelve dan, depending on the school of the dancer. The number of eight-beat patterns within each dan also varies, as does the exact order of the patterns used. The latter depends on the guild of the musicians. When we say, therefore, that we cannot provide a score of "the piece," any reader of the Interlude should not be surprised. The most specific information on the dance music is found in the textbook of the Komparu guild of taiko drumming, so let us begin there, with its comments on the flute part.

As noted earlier, the flute line generally serves as the basic guide for the structure of a noh dance. In the less secret pieces the flute music consists primarily of the four eight-beat melodic patterns mentioned in the Interlude (p. 44) plus special interjections of dan- or dance-identifying new patterns. I have found no printed versions of the flute music for the lion dance. However, the taiko instruction book does identify each dan of the dance by its name in flute music. The dan can in turn be subdivided into eight-beat segments of melodic units as in other flute pieces. Since the commercially available record of *Shakkyō* is of the Kanze school of noh, our abstraction of the flute music of the lion dance is based on the Kanze version of it, the order and names of each dan being derived from the Komparu guild taiko book.[37] The letters indicating each eight-beat unit represent a combination of information from the lectures of Professor Yokomichi Mario[38] and my own analysis of the recorded performance.

Every noh dance begins with a short opening (*kakari*) and has a closing (*tome*). Between these two sections there are five dan in the Kanze performance that can be outlined as follows:

kakari	A	B	A					
dan 1 (ji)	A	B	C	D	A			
dan 2 (kogaeshi)	A	B	B	C	D	A		
dan 3 (kan no te)	A'	V	V'	W	B	C	D	A
dan 4 (ryō no te)	A	X	X'	Y	C	D	A	
dan 5 (ōgaeshi)	A	B	B'	B'	C	D	A	
tome	A	Z	Z'	TK				

Looking over the entire structure, one observes the placement of the longest dan in the center and the most different melodic materials in the central dan (dan 3 and 4) and the finale. Dan 4 is unique, for the tempo suddenly slows down for units X and X', regaining speed in Y. The general titles of large (*ō*) and small (*ko*) *gaeshi* are clearly reflected in their lengths. Unit Z makes it evident that a closing (tome) and final cadence (kashira) are about to occur (thus the symbols TK). A comparison of the melodic units would show that they are more closely related than is revealed by their letter abstractions. Thus C really grows out of B, D is a slight variation on A, and V is based on the last notes of A'. Each dan begins and ends with A, and all dan conclude with the same three patterns (C D A). In all, the compactness of the structure is perhaps its most impressive characteristic.[39] With this as our introduction we can look now at the taiko music.

Since the flute *ji* (ground) dan is both literally and musically fundamental, we shall begin with the names of the drum patterns that accompany it according to the Komparu book:

A (8)	B (8)	C (8)	D (4)
ji = tsuke gashira	oroshi iroeji	iroeji	iroekake

E (8)	A' (4)
uchi kiri uchi kaeshi	kashira

The number of beats for each pattern is shown in parentheses to illustrate how the drum part is coordinated with the five eight-beat units of the flute part shown above. Letters have been assigned to the patterns to assist us in our discussion and to allow us to make comparisons with the flute and, later, the shamisen materials. Let us start with an abstraction of the taiko part that is comparable to that of the flute part:

kakari	B	DE	A′				
dan 1	A	B	C	DE	A′		
dan 2	A	B	C	C	DE	A′	
dan 3	A	B	C	C	C	C	DE A′
dan 4	A	C	C	C	C	DE A′	
dan 5	A	B	C	C	C	DE A′	
tome	A	Y	Z	A′			

The taiko and flute parts are obviously related structurally. In both parts, the first and last patterns of each dan are always the same, and the end of each dan uses the same set of three patterns (C DE A′ in the taiko dan). The internal structure of each taiko dan differs only in the order and number of repeats of patterns B and C. In the taiko part, as in the flute part, the most different materials are in dan 3 and 4 and the tome.

With such a seemingly restricted music one might wonder how one knows that the music is specifically for the lion dance. The order of sonic events is part of the answer. In addition, certain of the flute melodic units appear only in this piece. By the same token, taiko pattern B is reserved for use in lion dances. If one considers all the aspects of this one noh dance, one may understand how it is possible for hayashi musicians to play entire repertories without using notation. Even in such a restricted music, however, relativity has its place, as will be clear if we leave theory and turn to performance practice in the noh and kabuki versions of *Shakkyō*'s lion dance.

Examples 13a–e* show the basic taiko patterns for the lion dance as notated in the Komparu textbook.[40] The sonic difference between A and A′ is in the number of beats of silence, though the choreographic movements of the drumsticks during the first four beats of A are a distinctive difference to someone watching an actual performance. The "family" relation between B and C seems to be in the last four beats, whereas D is merely the first four beats of C. The rather long name of E reflects its ancestry, for it combines elements of two

separate, longer patterns. In all, it would seem relatively easy to
memorize all the patterns of the entire lion dance in order to listen to
or perform it accurately. However, one must stay loose. Example 13f
is a transcription of pattern B as it sounds on the Kanze recording. A
diligent reader might have already guessed that the taiko player is
not from the Komparu guild. He is a member of the Kanze guild of
drummers.[41] However, Example 13g is a transcription of the same
pattern in the same piece as played by a Komparu drummer on a
different Kanze school recording.[42] Alas, it also does not match up

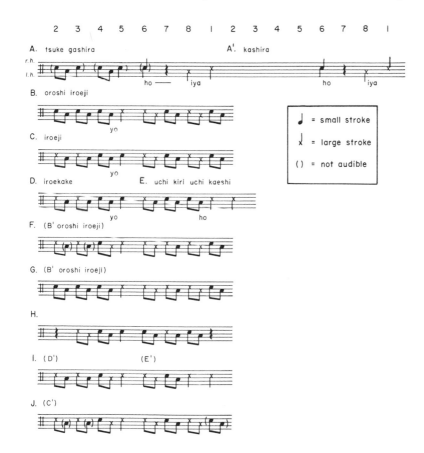

Example 13. Taiko patterns for the lion dance of *Shakkyō* (patterns in cassette examples K and L).

with the "correct" version B from the Komparu textbook, nor is it the same as that of the Kanze guild (Example 13f). What is the relevance of these differences to this study? They illustrate the relativity of notated resources in a world of aural, sometimes hidden, sonic events. The number of dan, the length of each dan, and the interpretation of each pattern within a dan are never improvised, but they are relative to a host of theoretical, musical, choreographic, and sociological factors that will shape them differently in ways that are distinct. Though this fact may confound a pragmatic researcher, it offers exceptional richness to one who remains flexible throughout this study. Let us keep that openness as we return to the nagauta version of *Shakkyō*.

Examples 13h and 13i show the two taiko patterns that are heard at the start of the shamisen line (Example 14a) in the nagauta equivalent of the lion dance heard on the recording (cassette example L). Example 13j is heard at the beginning of the second dan as marked in the shamisen notation.[43] If we take the dan markings from the shamisen line and use the equivalent letters for the taiko part (Example 13i = D′ and E, Example 13j = C′), we can construct the following outline of the taiko part for the nagauta lion dance:

dan 1   H D′ E A′ A
dan 2   C′ C′ D′ E A′ A
dan 3   C′ C′ C′ C′ D′ E A′ A
dan 4   V W C′ C′ D′ E A′ A
dan 5   C′ C′ C″ C″ D′ E A′ A″
tome   Y Z A′

Compare this with the outline of the noh taiko part on page 80. What first strikes the eye is the "misplacement" of pattern A. The pattern that signals an opening in noh occurs in nagauta as a closing. Both A and A′ have a cadential sound, but the location of the "end" of a dan in performance may be relative to the part to which one listens. In other words, we may have here an example of the sliding-doors effect mentioned in the Interlude (p. 42). The shamisen and hayashi are both playing eight-beat units, but they are not starting on the same first unit. For comparison's sake, let us move the kabuki drum patterns into a dan structure like that of the noh patterns on

page 80, rather than like that of the shamisen line with which the
nagauta taiko actually plays:

dan 1	H	D′E		A′			
dan 2	A	C′	C′	D′E	A′		
dan 3	A	C′	C′	C′	C′	D′E	A′
dan 4	A	V	W	C′	C′	D′E	A′
dan 5	A	C′	C′	C″	C″	D′E	A′
tome	A″	Y	Z	A′			

With this as a model, the similarities and differences in the noh and
kabuki taiko parts become quite clear. In the nagauta version, the
kakari and first dan are greatly truncated within one dan, but the
external units (A and D′E plus A′) remain stable. Dan 4 has quite
different units (V and W), just as did the flute at this point in the
noh version (p. 79). Recall also that in the noh version there was a
radical change of tempo here. A ritard may occur at this point in
some nagauta performances as well, but even without such an interpretation the thicker drum sounds of V and W are formally distinctive. The movement into the tome in the nagauta version is
slightly different, A″ being two kashira patterns in a row within one
eight-beat unit. This may be necessary because the shamisen normally drops out during the performance of the last three units (Y, Z,
and A′) of the tome section.[44]

Having compared the overall structure of the taiko music in the
two traditions, let us look once more at the individual patterns. We
have already noted how Example 13j relates to the noh *iroe* family
(compare with C), and how Example 13i relates to D and E and how
it also leads always to A′. However, Example 13h is bothersome.
Why such a radical difference? The answer is found by looking at the
shamisen phrase that the pattern accompanies (Example 14a). For
this short moment, the kabuki drummer has chosen to ignore the
conventions of noh and follow a kabuki tradition of directly supporting the rhythm of the melodic line. One can understand the importance of such support, as this is the opening phrase of a new section
of the composition that thereafter uses two kinds of music: kabuki
music in the melody and noh music in the hayashi. Once all has begun properly, the stylistic differences and sliding-doors effects can be

performed with confidence. Of course, we are dealing with only one example of a nagauta performance. The hayashi musicians are members of the Mochizuki guild. The same first dan looks somewhat different in the notation of the Semba guild.[45] Instead of a kabuki-style imitation of the shamisen line, we find a B pattern minus the first beat followed by D, E, and A'. This difference is particularly useful to us because it illustrates that the two major hayashi characteristics noted in our noh version can be found in kabuki as well, namely, (1) the use of named, stereotyped patterns in relatively set orders and (2) the existence of guild-generated differences in both the sounds and the formal ordering of such patterns.

In our comparative study we looked at only half of the hayashi materials, for a similar study of the ō and ko tsuzumi music would be intellectually redundant. The overall guiding principles of such music in both noh and kabuki should now be clear. However, we cannot leave this section of *Shakkyō* without looking at the unique kabuki addition to the music, the shamisen.

In the shamisen notation, this section is called a mad (*kurui*) interlude (*ai no te*) rather than a lion dance. Example 14a* is a transcription of the first dan of the shamisen music. In the context of our previous studies of the hayashi music, one can first note the rigid eight-beat lengths of each phrase (if one counts the opening rest of the first phrase). The four phrases of the first dan have been given letters by the author to allow us to compare the five dan of the shamisen line with the dan that we have abstracted earlier.

dan 1   A B C D
dan 2   E A B C
dan 3   D'F G H A B C D
dan 4   I J K A B C D
dan 5   L K'M A B C D

Compare this abstraction with that of the noh-flute line (p. 79). The sameness of dan cadences is the most obvious similarity, and the greater use of new material and new dan beginnings in the shamisen line the major difference. Shamisen interludes in general are often much freer in both the variety of their melodic units and the length of their phrases, but one senses a structural inspiration from the noh tradition in this music. The use of a varied D as a transition between dan 2 and 3 [46] reflects a kabuki, not a noh, technique. Example 14e* shows this opening phrase of the third dan. Note that it contains a modulation to the "radical" miyako tetrachord (see p. 40). Perhaps this represents a "hidden" influence of noh, for a study of noh dance music will reveal that a new melodic element often appears some three-fifths into the piece (see dan 3 on p. 79).

Our brief study of the shamisen part seems to reveal a clear compromise between noh and kabuki elements. We cannot leave this example, however, without commenting on its relation to other kabuki lion-dance music. Example 14b* is a transcription from a *jiuta* 1738 *Shakkyō* derived from the dance piece *Tuskai jishi*.[47] Cassette example M includes an excerpt from the 1754 nagauta piece *Shujaku shishi*[48] that is not notated as it is the same melodically as Example 14b except for an opening quarter note B and a B for the E in measure 2. Example 14c* is from the 1861 nagauta lion piece *Renjishi*.[49] Historically, Example 14b represents the two oldest surviving eighteenth-century shamisen-related lion-dance pieces. The *Shakkyō* of this study in Examples 14a and 14e was created in 1820 and Example 14c was next. Example 14d* follows with an excerpt from an 1878 piece to be discussed below. Two major points seem evident from this comparative score and its chronology. First, note the degree to which each subsequent "new" composition kept essential melodic elements of the original shamisen piece in at least the opening of the interlude. Second, we can conclude that if the formal structure of the noh flute music influenced the style of this shamisen interlude, it seems to have done so in the very first shamisen pieces (Example 14b). The evidence of such an influence emerges if one compares the shamisen music in cassette example M with the flute melody of noh-drama lion dance in cassette example K. While the pitches are different, the contour of the flute line seems to be the hidden guide for the construction of the shamisen melody.

The reader may now be flexible enough to be prepared for different materials as the history of one composition progresses. In this spirit, the "New Shakkyō" (*Shin-shakkyō*) nagauta piece of 1878 is most revealing. If one listens to the instrumental interlude in the position comparable to that of the lion dance in the earlier *Shakkyō*

Example 14. Shamisen versions of the kurui interlude from the nagauta *Shakkyō* (14a and 14e in cassette example L, 14b–d in cassette example M).

compositions, *Shin-shakkyō* is noteworthy in the fact that it does *not* use elements of Example 14 in the shamisen line at that time. However, the taiko accompaniment uses patterns like those shown in Example 13 and in the same general progressions while the rest of the hayashi is equally similar. Apparently new leaves do not change their roots but rather communicate new color on old branches. The position of the branch may also change, for a study of the entire piece *Shin-Shakkyō* reveals that the complete lion hayashi accompaniment has already been used earlier in an instrumental interlude before the kudoki section. As seen in Example 14d*,[50] there are as well, at this point, slight references in the shamisen line to melodic units of the lion dances of the earlier pieces. Both this interlude and the later one end in the style of the lion dances, the shamisen dropping out while the hayashi plays its tome. Thus the new *Shakkyō* refers directly to the lion dance of the noh hayashi on two occasions, covering the first occasion with shamisen material that relates to known kabuki lion dances and cloaking the second in quite new melodic material.

We have spent a considerable amount of time on various aspects of the lion-dance section of *Shakkyō* not only because it represents the climax of the composition but also because it is so rich in examples of principles that are essential to the hidden meanings of noh and kabuki music. With these principles in mind, we can discuss the finale of the composition more succinctly.

THE CHIRASHI AND DANGIRE (KIRI)

The standard transition from a noh dance to the finale section of a play is the entrance of the chorus with a repeated line. This is maintained in the nagauta version, as seen in lines 87 and 88. In both the noh and the nagauta version the flute enters briefly between the two lines, but the singers carry the melodic line thereafter. In both compositions the drums of the hayashi continue to play noh patterns. They are set in a conventional order for this section of a noh play. In the context of our previous study of the taiko part during the lion dance, perhaps the most significant observation is that patterns B and C are *not* used in the center of each dan.[51] The experienced listener will be receiving reassuring signals that the final dance is in progress. The nagauta composition maintains eight-beat phrases in the shamisen line as a kabuki overlay on noh hayashi music.

In both the noh and the nagauta composition, the text is chanted rather syllabically to create a dense but not unnecessarily hurried texture. There are more lines in the noh text than in the nagauta version, but text setting as such is not a major consideration in either tradition at this point. The nagauta music requires no additional references to the ōzatsuma recitative style, as the music is filled with drum and shamisen sounds and rhythms, though ōzatsuma tonalities appear for line 96, when plants bend. In the noh drama the flute returns as the chorus chants the last line while the drums play cadencing patterns. The entire play then ends with two solo strokes on the taiko. The nagauta ending is equally true to its convention. The hayashi stops before the beginning of the last line, the tempo becomes rubato, the noh flute returns, and after the last, slow syllable of the text the shamisen and hayashi join in a common final stroke.

In our first search for hidden traditions in music of Japan, the similarities and differences between a noh and a kabuki setting of the same story have given us specific examples of the basic principles that we sought. Of course, there is still more to be said about noh and kabuki music, but perhaps enough has been revealed here that some musical guideposts will be available if one chooses to travel further into this large and interesting repertory.

Kanda matsuri, Festival Music in a Nagauta Concert Piece— Two Genres in One Composition

Rᴇᴀᴅᴇʀs who have followed our first three studies should be aware that one must adopt a flexible attitude if one is to view Japanese music in a Japanese perspective. In the last view, we saw how one story, *Shakkyō*, looked very different when seen in two different genres, noh and nagauta. Here we shall see how two different idioms, shamisen and festival music, are combined in one nagauta composition, *Kanda matsuri*. However, let us begin with a history of the piece and of its topic.

Kanda matsuri, "The Kanda Festival," was composed in 1911 by Yoshizumi Kosaburō IV (1876–?) and Kineya Rokushirō III (b.

1874) using a text by Kodo Tokuchi (d. 1913).[1] A dance piece by the
same name had been written in 1839 in the *kiyomoto* genre of shamisen music for use in the theater. However, the nagauta composition
was created for a very different purpose. It was written in celebration
of the one-hundredth concert performance given by the Kensei kai
school of nagauta music.[2] The two composers of the piece had helped
to found the Kensei kai school in 1902. The major purpose of this
school was to meet the modern music world with new compositions
in traditional idioms. Both men had been professional kabuki theater musicians, but they later became concerned with the development of nagauta in a concert rather than a theater context. Actually,
such a movement had been active for nearly one hundred years, the
first official concert (ozashiki) nagauta piece being the 1820 composition *Oimatsu* by Kineya Rokusaburō IV (1779?–1855).[3] Thanks
to a continued compositional effort there is now an impressive list of
concert nagauta. Many have become as much a part of the contemporary nagauta performance and recording repertory as are the dance-
accompaniment pieces for the kabuki and dance stages.[4] Among
them, *Kanda matsuri* is one of the best contributions of the early
twentieth century.

The topic of *Kanda matsuri* was certainly appropriate to the cele-
brative purpose of its first performance, for the Kanda matsuri (festival) and Sannō matsuri are the two major festival processions of
Tokyo.[5] In the nineteenth and early twentieth centuries they com-
peted in popularity and opulence with the more famous Gion festival of Kyoto.[6] Historically, such festivals were believed originally
to have been ritual protections against illness and bad fortune. However, all three festivals developed into grand processions of digni-
taries, floats, and music or dance ensembles (see Figures 17, 18, and
20). Though these festivals still generate from the Shinto shrines
after which they are named, the efforts of local wards and businesses
give them a secular aura that is best understood by patrons of the
various parades that take place before the New Year's football bowl
games in America. Note, in Figure 17, that bleachers were arranged
along the route of the Kanda festival so that thousands of viewers
could enjoy the event and local shops could prosper from the resul-
tant tourist industry.

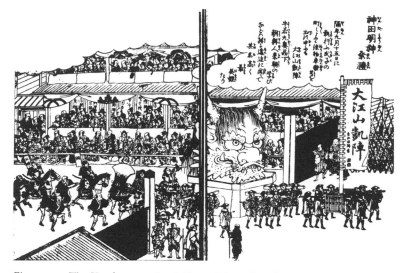

Figure 17. The Kanda processional. From *Edo meisho zukai*.

The Kanda matsuri traditionally is held on the fifteenth day of the ninth month and is associated with the Kanda Myojin Shinto shrine in the Kanda area of Chiyoda-ku in Edo (Tokyo). Its festive nature made it an ideal topic for a nagauta congratulatory composition. In addition, we should note that the Tokyo audiences for whom the composition was written were familiar with the Kanda event and thus could better appreciate the moods and meanings of the music and text. This is particularly significant when we recall that *Kanda matsuri* was a concert piece, and thus no dancers were present to help clarify the meaning of the work. What is of special interest in this study is the manner in which the musicians have integrated Edo festival sounds and spirit with the conventions of nagauta composition. We shall look at the text first to understand the overall intent and structure of the piece and then, using the text as our guide, turn to the music itself.

The terms of the kabuki dance form discussed in the Interlude have been used to divide the text. However, most of these terms do not appear in the actual text or printed music of the piece. Thus these formal divisions should be considered as presumptions of the author based on a study of the musical content of the piece and a familiarity with the tradition. A Western reader might understand this method of dividing if he thinks of pieces in sonata-allegro form in which an informed listener does not need to see the terms *development* and *recapitulation* on a score in order to recognize their location. The formal terms in parentheses are derived from the festival music tradition; their use will become evident in the analysis that follows. It must be remembered that any viable music tradition is open to innovation and change. The "new" nagauta of the early twentieth century, performed in a concert hall, should be expected to demonstrate some of this creativity. *Kanda matsuri* will not fail us in this regard. But first let us read the text.[7]

KANDA MATSURI

Maebiki, Oki

1.	Kanda matsuri o matsuyoi no	Waiting for the Kanda matsuri in the early evening,
2.	mikisho ni iketa myōto-bana	with the sacred wine are placed a pair of flowers.
3.	taga tezusabi ka shiragiku to	Who has arranged them? The white chrysanthemum
4.	kigiku no tsuyu mo atarashiku	and the yellow one too, freshly bedecked with dew,
5.	kazaru meika no kin byōbu	are like a master artist's gold folding screen.
6.	yukikai shigeki tsuji tsuji ni	Coming and going are crowds of people at every corner.
7.	kasane-kotoba mo kiki nareta	The repeated phrases one hears have become familiar sounds.
8.	gosairei omatsuri banzuke	"Programs for the grand festival!"
9.	yatsuya tōri ni Kawaru Bunbuku Chagama	On Eighty-eighth Street the Magic Kettle of Fortune—
10.	nanatsu no kane wa itsu tsuita yara	who knows when the seven bells rang?

Michiyuki
(Shoden)

11.	Honobono to shirami watarite tōtenkō	Faintly, the dim light of morning sweeps across the reddening eastern sky
12.	ichibandori wa taihei no	as the first cockcrow sounds its omen

13. miyo o iōte koke musu kanko | for a peaceful reign with a moss-covered drum.
14. niban no hoko wa Barekijin | The second float is the Protective God of Horses.
15. masaru medetaki shōzobu eboshi | What exquisite ceremonial robes and courtly headgear!
16. don don kakka don kakka | Boom-boom, rat-a-tat. Boom, rat-a-tat.

(Ai)

17. tsuzuku sanban shiki toshite | The third one follows according to schedule.
18. Okina no dashi wa Kanda Maru | It is the float of the elders called Kanda Maru.
19. goban jūban tsugi tsugi ni | The fifth one! The tenth one! On and on they come.

Ai no Te
(Yatai)

20. Machi nenban no tsuke matsuri | The special music and dances of town after town,
21. Sumiyoshi odori daikagura | the Sumiyoshi dance, shrine festival music,
22. yatai bayashi wa Yoshizumi to | festival cart music; Yoshizumi and Kineya
23. Kineya ga mochi no kikygasane | are wearing white costumes with dark red linings—
24. shomō | play it!
25. shomō ni tekomai no | The performers respond to the requests of the
26. tateshu ga ō no koe ni tsure | bystanders watching the festival dances by striking up
27. wataribyōshi o uchi agete | the processional beat to the shouts of approval from the onlookers.

(Wataribyōshi)
Kudoki

28. Mukashi yori koi to iu ji wa | From the first time, long ago, when someone first wrote
29. taga kakisomete mayoi no tane o | the word called "love," it has been sowing seeds
30. makinuran ahinobu no wa | of temptation and doubt. In the dark of night
31. kaze mo fuki sōrō ame mo furi sōrō | the winds blow, the rains fall,

32. niku ya togamuru sato no inu — and spite is inflamed by spies in the brothel.

Odori Ji

33. Magaki ni yotte hoto hoto to — They meet by the fence, and because they strike it off

34. tatakeba kiku ni okiamaru — so well they stay too long in the chrysanthemums.

35. tsuyu wa parari to mina chirinuredo — And although the dew is all scattered in large drops

36. onaji omoi ni machi wabishi — they wait impatiently with the same desires.

37. hime wa toboso ni tate idete — The young lady starts to go towards the gate

38. iza konata e to tomonaeri — and saying, "Come on, this way," they leave together.

39. yo kaze ni onmi mo hienuran — In the evening wind my body will not grow cold

40. kokoro bakari ni habere domo — even though I am all alone with only my heart beside me.

41. warawa ga mōke no kiku no sake — I offer a toast with ceremonial chrysanthemum wine,

42. kikoshimese ya to sakazuki no — and raising the wine cup I say, "Have a drink!"

43. kazu kasanareba uchi tokete — As the number of cups piles up, inhibitions are cast off

44. ai to ai to no aioi renri — and love with love is intertwined in mutual love.

45. yoso no miru me mo urayamashi — The eyes of others are filled with envy.

(Shichōme)

46. Ato no shomō wa eshaku naku — Wanting to do something else he leaves without a bow

47. suban no dashi ni oware owarete — and rushes off chasing after the numerous festival floats.

Ai no Te
(Kiyari)

48. Ōnyāryōi — Yo-heave-ho!

49. kogane hana saku yutaka na miyo ni sore — The golden flowers bloom for a prosperous reign. Look out!

50. shimero yare nakazuna — Tie up the middle rope!

51. ēnyāryōi — Yo-heave-ho!

Chirashi

52. Date mo kenka mo Edo no
    hana

For wooing as well as quarreling
the flowers of Edo

53. sono hanagasa no saki soro

are blooming on that flower-
adorned hat.

54. sakura no baba e dōdō to

The light of the setting sun shines
brightly upon the crowd

55. yosekuru hito no nami ma yori

of people approaching the Cherry
Grounds with festive pomp and
excitement.

Dangire

56. hikari mabayuku noboru hi no
    kage

The shadows of night fall.

A few comments on the text are in order before we begin musical
analysis. Its poetic structure is fairly traditional, consisting mostly
of units of seven or five syllables.[8] If there is a modernity to the text
it may be in the fact that one has a sense of the action from its reading alone. Traditionally nagauta was classified as a lyrical rather than
a narrative genre.[9] Since nagauta originated as dance accompaniment, its texts tended to be a mosaic of images or tableaux, the choreography carrying the burden of the story. Even in dance pieces the
text and choreography seldom gave a clear picture of a plot or story.
The audiences of the times usually knew the story source behind the
dance. Thus the evocation of some particular action or mood occurred in the observer's mind rather than on the stage. However,
since the mid nineteenth century there had been several attempts in
concert nagauta to produce pieces with dialogues and other story elements that are found in the narrative genres of shamisen music.[10]
Kanda matsuri does not go that far, but the actions underlying its
lyricism are unusually clear. The first ten lines evoke the setting of
the Kanda area before the festival parade begins; they describe deco-
rations that one would find in a Shinto shrine area at festival time,
mention the crowd, give the call of the program hawkers, and name
a local symbol of good fortune.[11] By nagauta standards this is a
rather detailed text. The style is maintained in lines 11–27, which
describe the actual parade. At first, lines 28–45 seem curiously out
of keeping with the topic of the piece. However, they fit in several

Figure 18. Floats in the Kanda festival. From *Ichiju saihoin hitsu*.

ways. We noted in Figure 17 the many people observing the parade from bleachers or second-story windows. The latter were often in teahouses or brothels, so that indoor pleasures could easily interrupt one's attention to the events outside. Thus a party interlude during the festival is sociologically correct. The change in subject of this section also shows the influence of traditional kabuki dance form. The kudoki, by tradition, is the most lyrical and sensual section of a nagauta composition. Such a mood would be hard to create in the context of the festival itself. The fact that love leads to more activity and drinking in lines 33–45 also reflects a proper sectional change of mood, for the odori ji often contains a lyrical but more active dance in a standard nagauta piece. Lines 46–47 are perhaps the most radi-cal in that they actually tell us that a man left the pleasures of an inner garden to view the festival once more. Lines 48–51 are a clear evocation of the firemen acrobats and their songs. As for lines 52–56, a look at Figure 18 will show that masses of flower-adorned hats are part of the festival. Furthermore, in pre-streetlight eras the pro-cession had to be completed by sunset, and thus the composition fittingly ends with nightfall.

To appreciate how modern the text is, one would have to compare it with traditional examples.[12] However, we shall rely on the music itself to learn about new traditional music in Japan.

THE OKI

The shamisen part in the opening section of *Kanda matsuri* has been transcribed in Example 15* to show the mixture of traditional and modern musical styles that is part of twentieth-century nagauta.[13] The shamisen prelude is meant to capture the exciting mood of the Kanda area before the procession begins. The wide skips in the shami-sen line are not exceptional, but their combination with the fast tempo is, perhaps, an attempt to evoke the kind of instrumental vir-tuosity that was more characteristic of the late-nineteenth-century European music that was being heard in Japan at the time this work was composed.[14] To the traditional ear, such an instrumental open-ing (*maebiki*) might sound rather modern. Its fast tempo continues through the first nine lines of text, so that they, too, move at a speed

Example 15. The shamisen oki section of *Kanda matsuri* (cassette example N).

appropriate to the excitement of the moment. However, it is really too fast for traditional dance accompaniment. Thus, the composition has begun with a clear musical statement that it is a concert piece, not a kabuki dance.

Another implication of modernity in *Kanda matsuri* is found in its approach to tonality as revealed in the setting of the first ten lines of the text. Nothing is unorthodox about the choice of tonal centers or the creation of melodic tension by means of pauses on upper or lower leading tones of such centers. What is striking is the density of such events and the changes of register. Figure 19 shows an outline of the basic tonal centers of this section; their octaves are indicated by lowercase and capital letters. Every line of text starts with a modulation from the last tonal center of the previous line, and there are tonal changes within each line except the eighth and the last. Line 8 is the street cry of the program sellers and thus is accompanied by a tonally static ostinato. The last line logically slows both tempo and modulatory tendencies to create a sectional cadence.

The shifts of pitch center relate to yet another important element in shamisen music, namely, modulations in terms of the tetrachords shown in Example 2. The movement in measures 20–34 from E to B to A is a good case in point. The first phrase (mm. 20–28) gives us only E and F-sharp. With such little information one cannot say with authority whether F-sharp is the upper leading tone of E or E is the lower leading tone of F-sharp. The next phrase opens (mm. 29–31) with miyako tetrachords, one on F-sharp and one on B, but then moves on (mm. 31–34) through a minyō tetrachord on B to a miyako tetrachord on A. To analyze this in terms of the yo and in scales is to use measuring tools too long to fit the units actually present. The tetrachordal analysis seems to provide a clearer picture of the modulatory dynamics of the music.

The effectiveness of upper or lower leading tones as means of generating melodic tension is evident if we study phrases like those in measures 44–52 and 57–62. Note that every quarter note that is followed by a rest is an upper or lower leading tone to E, B, or F-sharp. These devices for continual melodic flow and tension during silence can be seen in most of the phrases that follow in the example.

Traditionally, there is an inverse ratio between rhythmic activity in a shamisen line and its melodic tension. This holds true for most of the oki section of *Kanda matsuri*. However, its fast tempo places tonal tensions in a uniquely close temporal relation. Study Example 15 and Figure 19 with this tempo in mind or listen to cassette example N and you will become aware of the speed with which the register of the shamisen line changes. Note, for example, the movement from the highest pitch in measure 58 to the lowest in measure 78. It is important to recall that the musical characteristics mentioned are not by themselves unorthodox. It is the combination of these characteristics here that is stylistically challenging, and makes the music as colorful as the scene it is meant to represent. The

Text line	Measures	Tonal outline
1	19–31	E-B
2	32–46	E-A-b-e
3	47–56	f♯-b-e
4	57–78	B'-F♯-E-b-e-b'
5	79–98	e-E-b-e
6	99–113	b-E-b
7	114–122	F♯-b-e
8	123–132	b
9	133–152	E-b-E
10	153–163	b-b

Figure 19. Modulations in the oki of *Kanda matsuri*.

change in tempo at measure 153 and the "half cadence" feeling of the concentration on B skillfully lead us out of the mood of the oki and towards the change of shamisen tuning and style for the next section.

THE MICHIYUKI

The next section of *Kanda matsuri* opens with a change of the shamisen tuning to *ni agari* (raising the middle string a whole step to F-sharp). While changes of tunings in nagauta dance pieces are quite common, they do not normally occur so early in the form. Recall that the michiyuki section usually implies the entrance of some important figure. In *Kanda matsuri*, the text of this section (lines 11–19) parades the floats before us (Figure 18). To enhance this picture, the hayashi does not use the instruments of the traditional kabuki

Figure 20. A yatai cart. From *Kanda myojin sairai gyōretsu emaki*.

theater but rather those of the festival ensembles (*matsuri bayashi*) found on the floats themselves. These consist of a bamboo flute (takebue or *yokobue*), taiko and *ōdaiko* stick drums, and a hand gong (*kane* or *atarigane*). Figure 20 shows such an ensemble on a float (*yamadashi*) of the type described in the text. Note that the bird described in line 12 also refers to the phoenix or the crane seen in Figure 20. The drum of line 13 is not a festival drum but rather a reference to a Chinese tale about a drum left outside the palace that could be sounded whenever a citizen had a complaint he wished to address to the emperor.[15] Naturally, moss grew over its unused skin.

The mixture of the sounds of the festival ensemble with those of the shamisen piece may puzzle a Western listener. One gets the impression from Example 16* that the drums support the shamisen line rhythmically in a random fashion and that the rhythmic patterns and density of the gong are quite different from those of the shamisen or the drums. Though the flute part does pause on some pitches also found in the shamisen line, its melodic style between these pitches seems quite independent even in tonal system (note the cross relation in m. 12). In another recorded performance of *Kanda matsuri* the flute player enters earlier (in m. 7) and plays a very different melodic line, and the gong part is much simpler.[16] One might conclude that, as in some Charles Ives compositions, two kinds of music are going on at one time. This is in fact part of what is happening. Let me explain.

First let us recall our earlier discussion, at the end of the Interlude, of the nagauta compositional process. Since different guilds may be involved in different performances, one may expect variations such as are found in the flute part in the performances discussed above. However, this does not explain the internal discrepancies that seem to exist. The flute part shown in Example 16 could be understood as combining the highly ornamenting style (*ashirai*) of bamboo flutes found in the lyrical sections of other nagauta compositions[17] with sounds that help to create the atmosphere implied by the text. Since flutes are part of the ensembles used in the procession, some reference to their sound is a logical part of the orchestration at this point in the composition. A comparison of the flute line with an actual festival melody shows that while it is not a specific festival tune, its ornamentations are similar in style to those of professional festival flute music.[18] The ambiguity of the flute part and its resulting indistinct line are necessary in order that it not interfere with the shamisen and vocal lines that are the core of the composition.

The gong part reflects typical festival music patterns,[19] in, for example, measures 10 and 11. At the same time it is influenced by the rhythm of the shamisen part, as seen in measure 12. The drum parts, however, remain a puzzle. While one could conjure up subtle rhythmic relations between the drum parts and that of the shamisen, they would reflect, I feel, more the imagination of the Western-style analyst than the intent of the Japanese compositional commune. The secret clue to the musical structure is found by studying the subject of the text and the musical traditions it implies. Since the text is about a procession, the drummers are playing an actual festival piece, *Shoden*. They have chosen one of the slower festival pieces because of the ponderous nature of this part of the parade, with its huge, heavy floats pulled by oxen or groups of men. The bottom line of Example 16 is a standard version of the drum patterns for *Shoden* as taught to a beginner.[20] With it as a guide we can clearly understand the drum parts of the nagauta piece. The actual Kanda festival version of *Shoden* in cassette example P helps us remember the importance of variants in understanding the use of such traditional material.[21] The two transcribed versions of *Shoden* are nearly identical and the recorded version is similar. We have a clear case of two kinds of music going on at the same time, and we also have a good reason for their combination in the scene they represent. The flute and gong parts are a compromise between the demands of the two types of music. Note, for example, the unusual gong pattern on the second beat of measure 26. These unique sixteenth notes with an open sound (*chon chon*) occur on precisely the first beat of the repeat of the *Shoden* drum piece, thus showing that the gong player is aware of the phrasing of both the shamisen and the drum parts. This brings us to yet another fascinating aspect of Japanese polyphony. The two kinds of music are not using the same beat 1. As notated, the shamisen period consists of sixty-four beats set in thirty-two measures of 2/4 time. It was pointed out in the Interlude that the implied strong-weak accents of this form of Western notation are not necessarily those of Japanese music, even when written with such a graphic crutch. Nevertheless, the phrasing of the shamisen line does fit neatly into the Western notational design. As shown in Figure 21, the phrases of the shamisen part are mostly in twelve- or eight-beat lengths. The drum piece *Shoden* begins with an eight-beat pattern and then goes into repeats of a thirty-two-beat unit. However, as seen in Example 16 and Figure 21, these symmetrical drum units do

Example 16. A comparative score of the opening of the michiyuki from *Kanda matsuri* and the matsuri bayashi piece *Shoden* (*Kanda matsuri* michiyuki in cassette example O, festival variant of *Shoden* in cassette example P).

not begin on the same first beat as those of the shamisen symmetrical phrases. Of course, one can continue to question the location of beat "1" in any Western notation or analysis of non-Western music (as well as in much Western music). Perhaps the most fruitful view of such ambiguous designs is that derived from the concept of relativity. The placement of beat 1 is seen differently by the two groups of musicians involved. The result is the sliding-doors effect discussed earlier: internally symmetrical units (often in multiples of four) are begun on different beats of a common time frame. As seen in Figure 21 and Example 17*, the sliding-doors discrepancy is maintained until the last unit, at which time an extra beat is added to the shamisen melody so that the shamisen and drum parts will reach the final cadence (m. 68) at the same moment. The drum "coda" of this piece is not the one known to me, though, as in most festival versions of *Shoden*, it is shorter than the thirty-two-beat unit. A comparison of the coda in Example 17 with the full drum pattern in Example 16 shows that the coda drumming consists of beats 4−10 plus beats 1−7 of the full pattern, with beat 10 of the first unit overlapping with beat 1 of the second. It remains conjectural whether the shamisen line is adjusting to the percussion line in this passage

Example 17. The final unit of michiyuki and the first of kangen in *Kanda matsuri* (final unit at the end of cassette example O, kangen in cassette example Q).

FIGURE 21

Measure |11| |25| |33| |37| |43|
Shamisen | 12 | 8 | 8 | 8 | 12 | 8 | 8 | 8 | 12 | 12
DRUMS | (11) | 8 | 32 | | 32 | 32

M |49| |54| |58| |64|
SU | 10 || 8 | 8 | 4 | 9 | (3) || = 138
DU _____|_____ 20 _____| (3)   = 138

Figure 21. A comparative chart of the michiyuki of *Kanda matsuri* and the festival piece *Shoden*.

or whether the percussion line is adjusting to the shamisen line. In any case, the overall passage is an excellent example of the manner in which temporal disjunctions between time units are used to give the music a strong sense of forward motion towards a cadence.

As the second float comes into view (line 14), the shamisen play a melodic pattern known as *kangen* (mm. 70–74 in Example 17). This pattern is used in many nagauta pieces to suggest court ensemble music and is probably used here to add grandeur to the procession.[22] Such an ensemble (gagaku) does not normally appear in such festivals, though their instruments have been used in recent years in Shinto processions. In the orchestration of the *Kanda matsuri* recording, one hears in this section widely separated sounds of a large odaiko drum as the ones seen on the festival floats (Figures 18 and 20). This drum adds another true festival sound, and contributes to the ponderous effect desired for this passage. Line 16 of the text contains the mnemonics for the sounds of the drum as it is struck on the head and the rim. In performances these are often paralleled by the same sounds on the drum itself.

A shamisen and ōdaiko interlude leads next to a section in a livelier tempo as new floats pass by. Example 18* shows the opening of this section. The shamisen rhythm of measures 5–8 is significant because it implies the rhythm of the drum pattern that follows (mm. 9–12). This drum pattern is known variously as *torikagura* (bringing out of a Shinto theatrical) or *uchi kome* (playing out). It is a standard opening pattern for many of the faster festival ensemble pieces. In the light of our previous analysis, the relation of the shamisen and drum parts in the music that follows is of particular interest. Note in measures 17 and 18 that when the festival music really begins,

Example 18. Uchi kome or torikagura passages in *Kanda matsuri* (cassette example R).

the drums start two beats before the shamisen, thus setting up once more a sliding-doors effect.

The mention of Okina in line 18 evokes in Japanese minds the image of a famous old man's mask dance that is part of most Shinto congratulatory ceremonies and is seen in the noh and kabuki at the beginning of every year or theater season. The term *Kanda Maru* in line 18 refers to a float, but it is also the name of a drum pattern used by various festival groups, and the term used by offstage (geza) musicians in the kabuki when they are playing music in a festival style.[23] Both these traditions are characterized by the kind of dialogue, or call and response, between two drums seen in Example 18. Thus the setting of this moment in *Kanda matsuri* is appropriate: it carries a hidden sonic message of which listeners may not be consciously aware, though they may react unknowingly to the aptness of the music. In a similar, covert manner listeners might sense the approach of an important cadence in the setting of line 19, for the tension of the disjunct, sliding-doors phrasing has been removed. It is completely gone in the first seven measures of Example 19, the heavy emphasis on one rhythm being used as a signal that a new mood and style are coming in the next section of the piece.

THE AI NO TE (*YATAI*)

The two terms with which we have labeled this section both appear in the shamisen notation. Recall that *ai no te* means an instrumental interlude and is a common feature of nagauta in both dance and concert forms. The word *yatai* is the name of a cart that is used in festivals to pull ensembles of musicians through the streets (Figure 20), and *yatai bayashi* (line 22) means the playing of the piece *Yatai* that generally opens and closes suites played by festival hayashi (cassette example S). This concert interlude is related to the well-known festival piece in several ways. First, in most performances the shamisen line is supported by the drums, flute, and hand gong of the festival hayashi. Only the drum parts of the hayashi have been included in the transcription of Example 19 as they and the shamisen line are the least variable in recordings and performances. We noted earlier how, in the *Shoden* section, the hand-gong part tended to respond to the shamisen and drum lines whereas the bamboo flute played melodic units inspired more by the relevant festival melody than by that of the shamisen. This is the case as well in the *Yatai* interlude. The most obvious relation to the original festival piece is found in the drum parts in measures 9–16 of Example 19. The drummers are playing uchi kome, the traditional opening pattern for festival pieces mentioned earlier. At the same time the shamisen are playing direct rhythmic imitations of this pattern. To strengthen the festival associations these eight measures are repeated halfway through the interlude.

Having established that this interlude is in the festival style, we turn next to the question of its modernity. One might suspect a Western influence in the virtuosity of the shamisen part, though similar technical displays can be found in many premodern nagauta compositions.[24] When this style is combined with the tonal and

Example 19. The beginning of the *Yatai* interlude in *Kanda matsuri*.

rhythmic characteristics of the passage shown in Example 19, however, one senses once more a skillful balance of traditional and new
modes of composition. Take, for instance, the tonal implications of
the section transcribed. The first phrase (mm. 9–15) pounds F-sharp
into our ear, but F-sharp does not return until measure 36. Measures
17–24 emphasize C, the unresolved upper leading tone of B, but
what of all the E's? The ear had been prepared to hear them as a lower
leading tone of F-sharp. If they are so interpreted, measures 25–32
are truly intense, for no clear pitch center or fifth appears until measures 35–36. In all, this period demonstrates many of the principles
of tension and release and tonal relativity that were introduced earlier in the Interlude. The same can be said for the next sixteen measures (m. 37ff.), for they are in fact a transposition of measures
17–33 a fifth higher.

Rhythmic elements also contribute to the dynamic quality of this
interlude. Measures 17–20 of the shamisen line and their repeat use
a three-beat unit notated in a duple meter. These "syncopations" are
followed by a contracting ostinato (mm. 25–31). We shall discuss
the relationship of such notated examples to Japanese concepts of
music in time shortly, but at this point let us return to the question
of modernity. Again we are confronted with ambiguity. No single
element in the excerpt shown is clearly modern. However, as in the
opening of the composition, the density of tonal and rhythmic features seems to imply a twentieth-century approach to traditional
idioms of shamisen music. With that in mind, we should turn next
to the drum parts.

We have already noted the use of a festival drum pattern at the
opening of the interlude and its direct rhythmic imitation by the
shamisen. The drums and shamisen seem to continue this close
rhythmic relationship throughout the interlude. Indeed, what seems
unusual about this section, as compared to the previous section, is its
lack of a sliding-doors effect. Is this part of the price paid for Western
modernity? I cannot say, for the traditional nagauta repertory is large
and its rhythmic relations are varied. However, there are other rhythmic aspects of this section that imply that the music maintains a
balance between the new and the old. First there is the ambiguity of
rhythmic dominance. Is the shamisen part influencing the drum

parts or vice versa? An answer consistent with the concept of relativity that is essential to this book is that the influence is mutual. While the drum pattern of measures 17–20 is not as specific as the opening uchi kome, it is quite typical of festival style and thus seems to influence the shamisen line. One can divide both the drum and the shamisen parts into eight-beat units, but a closer look at the drum music shows that it consists of a sixteen-beat pattern (mm. 17–24) that is repeated while the shamisen move on to new melodic and rhythmic materials. Thus, there seems to be a mild independence of phrase units, though the surface rhythms do not conflict. For example, the third statement of the sixteen-beat drum pattern starts in measure 33, which is where a closing, eight-beat phrase in the shamisen line also begins. The drum pattern changes slightly in measure 36 (the second-beat, accented eighth notes become a quarter note) to mark the shamisen cadence in the "middle" of the drum pattern. Then in measures 41–44 the drums change to a cadence pattern so that they will "come out even" with the eight-beat phrases of the shamisen. Thereafter, drums and shamisen are in synchronization (m. 45ff.).

We find further support for our theory of rhythmic relativity if we turn to other recordings of the same piece. In one case[25] the drummers repeat the pattern of measures 25–28, thus starting the complete, sixteen-beat pattern four measures later than in the transcription shown in Example 19. This adjustment allows the drum pattern to cadence with the shamisen part throughout the passage shown and obviates the need for a separate eight-beat cadence pattern in measures 41–44. If this were Western music, one might ask which version of the drum parts is correct, but it should be obvious by now that in Japanese terms both are. The drummers have simply slid their unit along a parallel track into a different relation with the track movement of the shamisen. Since the drum parts are conceived of and learned as pattern units, such a change in interpretation is not hampered by notation.

Example 20* presents another interesting aspect of the rhythm of this instrumental interlude. The Westerner may be struck by the fact that measures 79–82 add up to seven beats. Equally impressive are the four statements of the three-beat syncopated pattern ♪ ♩ ♪ ♩. It all seems most modern. A Westerner might notate this passage using

Example 20. A special rhythmic passage in the shamisen part of the *Yatai* interlude in *Kanda matsuri* (cassette example T).

a heterometric solution with three measures of 3/4 starting with measure 79, but the notation shown is derived directly from the printed shamisen music.[26] We see a Japanese notator slipping an asymmetrical unit into the symmetrical graphic conventions of the West with little concern, for, as we have noted in the Interlude, a traditional Japanese musician conceives of music in terms of phrases rather than accented measures. As far as is known, drummers never use notation during a performance of this piece. On the basis of personal performance experience, I would say that this drum passage is most effectively learned and played simply by knowing the shamisen melody and following along with three repeats of a pattern mnemonically taught as *tere ts(u)ku ten* plus a cadential *tere ts(u)ku ten ten*. Such an aural-oral-kinetic learning process is part of the secret art of Japanese drumming. It also helps to explain the logic of avoiding score notations of Japanese music.

Line 20 of the text is set with slower, integrated shamisen and drum parts. The drums drop out at the final cadence so that new percussion sounds can be heard in the section that follows. This is necessary as the text now describes a different aspect of the festival. In addition to floats there are groups from various districts of Tokyo and elsewhere in Japan who participate in the Kanda parade with their own special music or dance. The Sumiyoshi dance mentioned in line 21 was one of the more popular festival dances throughout Japan. Generally, it is a circle dance performed around a large umbrella by dancers wearing large, flower-adorned hats.[27] The shamisen set the mood of this dance with the repeated pattern shown in Example 21a*. This is supported by the pattern *kyōgen gakko* played by the noh flute, the noh taiko, and the ōdaiko. This pattern is derived from the kabuki, not the noh, tradition, and its name refers to a small drum that is often carried by street dancers. Thus the color and hidden cultural message of the hayashi accompaniment of this passage are most appropriate. They are equally appropriate as support for the term *daikagura* in the text. This term can refer to the pantomime dances in Shinto shrines that are usually accompanied by the *kagurabue* flute (which in sound resembles the nōkan) plus the ōdaiko and a *daibyōshi* drum. However, the word *daikagura* also refers to processional lion dancers, jugglers, or acrobats. The music for these daikagura traditions today (cassette example V) combines shamisen with the hayashi mentioned above. Thus, the orchestration provides an "authentic" background for the scene evoked by the text. Example 21b shows the shamisen accompaniment for the words *yatai bayashi* of line 22. It does not attempt to imitate the colorful sounds of the piece *Yatai*, because the word refers to the general repertory of the ensembles that ride the carts (Figure 20). Besides, we have already heard a full instrumental interlude based on *Yatai*. What is perhaps of greater musical importance is the fact that a sud-

Example 21. Three shamisen excerpts from *Kanda matsuri* (21a and related street music in cassette examples U and V).

den intrusion into a more formal setting of this section is compositionally illogical. One could say that the shamisen line is rhythmically denser just before and during the singing of these words (see Example 21b), but the basic tempo and style must remain steady if one is to picture the stream of persons and dancers who are passing by in the procession. Among the participants, the poet has included the two composers (Yoshizumi and Kineya), dressed in formal Shinto rather than kabuki musicians' garb. In this way, the original purpose of the composition is not lost in the flurry of the Kanda festival.

The shout of line 24 is called out naturally and is followed by a melodic rendition of line 25. The hayashi continues to play variations of the kyōgen gakko pattern until the last two words of line 27. Example 21c shows the shamisen setting of lines 26 and 27. What first catches the eye (or ear) is the implication of an F-sharp pitch center and, again, the use of a melodically tense pitch (D) before the rests. The F-sharp has been important since the last word of line 23. In the passage shown, B and then C-sharp also become important. The excerpts in Examples 21b and 21c illustrate the use of rhythmic density and new tonal materials (the pitch C-sharp) to intensify the finale of this section of the piece. The last seven measures of Example 21c are of special interest, for the miyako tetrachord on B returns when the drum pattern *wataribyōshi* is mentioned, but the final cadence provides a fresh emphasis on C-sharp, its F-sharp reinforcement appearing on the last beat. Since the text is calling out for the performance of *uchi agete* (striking up) and wataribyōshi, the rhythm of the last bars of Example 21c is the same as that of the wataribyōshi pattern itself (cf. Example 19, mm. 13–15). The shamisen notation at this point instructs the hayashi to play the patterns wataribyōshi and uchi agete.[28] During this short hayashi interlude there is a change in the shamisen tuning to *honchōshi* (a fourth and a fifth). This prepares us for a change of mood and section.

THE KUDOKI

I have called this the kudoki section, though the printed shamisen music includes the term *odori ji* at this point. Such a presumption is based on the nature of the text and on the style of the music and its orchestration. Lines 28—32 are set without any hayashi accompaniment, and the shamisen line is deliberately sparse so that there is ample room for vocal lyricism. The excerpt in Example 22 could, without its text, be from almost any kudoki section in the nagauta repertory.[29] The text itself is in a typical romantic style of a kudoki section. From the text it is obvious that someone has left the distractions of the parade to enjoy another amusement for which Edo was equally famous.

Example 22. A kudoki-style shamisen passage in *Kanda matsuri*.

THE ODORI JI

The entrance of the taiko and noh flute in the interlude between lines 32 and 33 gives the texture of the music a more typical odori ji style. Since the love affair is going on against the background of the festival outside, one is tempted to read significance into the fact that the taiko and flute are playing the wataribyōshi pattern noted earlier but at half speed. Another possible reason for this slower pace is the fact that in a suite of festival music the quietest piece, *Kamakura*, usually appears at this time (see Second View, n. 14, p. 203, and Figure 22). Whatever its reason for being, the change of texture is very effective. Again in the tradition of an odori ji, the ō and ko

Example 23. Shamisen word painting in *Kanda matsuri* (cassette example W).

tsuzumi drums, entering with line 35, give kabuki-style rhythmic support to the shamisen line.[30] These drums cadence at the end of line 36, and the shamisen and voice seem to suggest the motion implied in lines 37–38 by performing in a constantly changing, almost parlando rhythm. A solo singer extends the words *yo kaze ni onmi* (in the evening wind my body) in an obviously sensual manner and then proceeds with one shamisen to render lines 39–40 in a parlando fashion. The tempo increases in lines 41–44, though with much rubato as the drinking and the emotions increase. Perhaps the shamisen accompaniment for line 41, shown in Example 23a*, evokes the slight tipsiness of the lover. The rhythmic drone on the words *kiku no sake* (chrysanthemum wine) is the only one in this period of the music. The accompaniment for the word *tokete* (to dispel, untie) shown in Example 23b* may be another case of word painting, its unusual rhythm representing the casting off of inhibitions. The entrance of all the singers at line 45 is a signal that another section of the piece has ended.

THE *SHICHŌME AND AI NO TE*

Lines 46–47 of the text take our anonymous lover back to the pleasures of the festival. To help the listener in this return the hayashi returns, this time using the drums, hand gong, and flute of the festival ensemble. The shamisen notation identifies this section as *Shichōme* (literally "Fourth Avenue"), the name of the fourth piece in traditional festival hayashi suites. The hayashi part does seem to be derived from Shichōme patterns. In an actual festival suite, this is the fastest and showiest of the pieces, though it may start off moderately. In the nagauta composition, one hears a moderate tempo that gradually increases. It never reaches the speed of festival *Shichōme*, though the shamisen line remains consistently dense. Perhaps the major function of this section is to help us (and the lover-drinker) move out of the backyard garden and party room to the more public pleasures of the street parade.

Following a short shamisen interlude after line 47, the festival drums enter with their own solo rendition of the opening pattern (uchi kome) of *Yatai* that was made familiar to the listener in the

Example 24. The return of *Yatai* in *Kanda matsuri* (cassette example X).

previous, large ai no te. Its appearance here is not only festive but
also appropriate to the order of events in a festival, as the last piece of
a matsuri bayashi suite is *Yatai*. The hayashi version of the opening
pattern is followed by the second large instrumental interlude for
shamisen and hayashi. The first shamisen phrase strengthens the relationship with the first *Yatai* by being precisely that of the first interlude transposed one step higher (cf. m. 9 of Example 19 and m. 9
of Example 24*). One might suspect a modern or Western influence
here, for by traditional standards the use of G-sharp as a pitch center
is quite radical. In other respects, however, the interlude's structure
is what might be called traditionally modern. The hayashi maintains
a conventional *Yatai*-like line throughout the interlude, interrupted
only by call-response exchanges like that shown in Example 24*.
Similar exchanges occurred in the first *Yatai* interlude, and, as in
that previous virtuosic interlude, the opening shamisen and drum
pattern returns about two-thirds into the music (Example 24, mm.
9–15). If one measures the phrase length in these two interludes as is
done in the following chart, the similarities of structure become
obvious.

Beats per phrase
First *Yatai*   16 16 16 8 16 16 16 8 / 16 8+17 16 16
Second *Yatai*   16 16 16 8 16 16 16 16 / 16 16 16 16 6

What does one see? The first *Yatai* has one unorthodox section,
shown earlier in Example 20, and the second *Yatai* is somewhat

longer, but the overall design is the same. Freshness is created by a
new tonality (G-sharp), while traditional "correctness" is achieved
by including a final *Yatai*. The six-beat ending of the second *Yatai*
could be regarded as consisting of eight beats if one added the two
silent beats commonly found at the end of a long phrase. In this
case, these are absorbed by a vocal entrance, which marks the start of
a new section and a new scene.

THE KIYARI

Line 48 is performed by an unaccompanied singer and is marked in
the notation as a *kiyari ondo*, a form of song performed by certain
guilds of carpenters or firemen and heard in cassette example Y. Such
groups are still a colorful addition to Japanese parades. They wear
special jackets, carry identifying poles, and often suspend tall lad-
ders in the middle of the street with ropes while some daredevil
member does acrobatic tricks at the top. As can be heard in cassette
examples X and Y, lines 48–51 are imitations of kiyari music.[31]
Lines 49 and 50 are supported by a slow-paced, ostinato-like shamisen line. An ōdaiko drum hits widely spaced accents to help evoke
the stately sound and tempo of such a section in the parade.

THE CHIRASHI AND DANGIRE

The text of this closing section combines both the romantic and the
festival elements of the composition. At the same time, the orchestration combines the festival hayashi and the kabuki ō and ko
tsuzumi drums to create an energetic finale (cassette example Z).
One first hears the same festival opening pattern shown in measures
9–15 of Example 19. A listener should be quite familiar with the
uchi kome pattern by this time and thus be able to respond to its
festive implications.[32] A connoisseur of nagauta will recognize as
well the stylistic characteristics of a chirashi section in standard
nagauta form. These include the faster tempo, the use of a full ensemble and all the singers, and the steady stream of syllables. Any
subtleties that may lurk in the text are pretty well lost, for the instrumental sounds usually overwhelm the vocal line in live performances, though engineers distort the natural state of the music in

the usual tradition of studio vocal recording. Thus the double meanings or word games of lines 52–53 are primarily for those who know the text. The flowers of Edo may be flowers or geisha, and we have already noted in our illustrations the flowered hats that are typical of Kanda matsuri participants. Line 52 is sung syllabically against a repeat of the uchi kome pattern by the shamisen and hayashi. The drums and shamisen then play a sixteen-beat interlude in the style of the *Yatai* sections heard earlier. The same style is used for three more sixteen-beat units that support the syllabic, static singing of lines 53–55. In all of these chirashi units, the shamisen and drums move in parallel phrases (there are no sliding-doors effects). This creates a solid, forward-moving texture of a type more familiar to Western musicians. The shamisen do not play the last two beats of each unit, but rhythmic drive is maintained by the drums, which play in a continuous festival style. At the end of line 55, these two beats are extended by a fierce drumroll, an obvious sign that a concluding section has been reached. This roll is followed by a completely standard dangire final cadence[33] as night falls in line 56, closing another festival day in Kanda and ending the composition.

By now the festival participants and the readers of this study should be fatigued. Both have gone through a long but exciting experience. In the context of our other views of Japanese music, what has been learned? The outline in Figure 22 may help us in our reply.

Looking first at the two formal outlines of the piece, one sees a skillful interlocking of the conventional elements of two traditions, the kabuki dance form and Tokyo festival music. Whether viewed separately or in combination, these units provide an excellent sense of orderly progression through sonically identifiable formal sections to a logical conclusion. A listener familiar with these two genres would be able to participate subliminally in this musical adventure through a process of anticipation and prediction without ennui, for the combination of the two traditions leaves ample room for musical surprises. This sense of change is enhanced by the variety of orchestrations noted in Figure 22. These orchestrations not only help to identify the changes of formal units but also provide an important degree of unity and variety in the timbre and sonic density of the overall composition. The transparent texture of shamisen and voice

A formal outline of *Kanda matsuri* (Figure 22), presented in three stacked blocks:

Text lines		1–10	11–16	17–19	20
Nagauta formal unit	maebiki	oki	michiyuki	uchi kome	ai no te
Festival formal unit			*Shōden*		*Yatai*
Orchestration	S	S, V	S, V, MB (TB)		S, MB
Shamisen tuning	honchōshi	ni agari			
Tonal outline	E-F♯-B		F♯-B-E	F♯-B-E-F♯	B
Approximate tempo	♩=192		♩=76	♩=88	♩=240

Text lines	21–26	27	28–32	33–34	35–38	39–45
Nagauta formal unit	daikagura		kudoki	odori ji		
Festival formal unit		wataribyōshi		*Kamakura*		
Orchestration	S, NK, T, OD		S, V	S, V, NK, T	S, V, O, K	S, V
Shamisen tuning	honchōshi	honchōshi				
Tonal outline	B-F♯-C♯-F♯	E	B			parlando
Approximate tempo	♩=100		♩=92	♩=104		

Text lines	46–47		48–51	52–55	56
Nagauta formal unit		ai	kiyari	chirashi	dangire
Festival formal unit	*Shichōme*	*Yatai*		*Yatai*	
Orchestration	S, V, MB (TB)	S, MB	S, V, OD	S, V, MB (TB)	
Shamisen tuning					
Tonal outline	E-B-E-G♯	C♯-F♯	F♯-B-F♯	F♯-B-F♯	B
Approximate tempo	♩=236		♩=76	♩=200	♩=88 ritard

Figure 22. A formal outline of *Kanda matsuri*. S = shamisen, V = voice, MB = matsuri bayashi, (TB) = takebue, NK = nōkan, T = noh taiko, OD = ōdaiko, O = ō tsuzumi, K = ko tsuzumi.

(S, V, lines 1–10) is thickened by the addition of a festival sound (MB, lines 11–16) that leads to purely instrumental music (S, MB). The voice returns with a different color in the instrumental accompaniment (lines 21–26) because the text deals with a different kind of festival scene. A short drum and flute interlude (wataribyōshi) leads back to voice and shamisen, which in turn are succeeded by yet another hayashi texture, and, after a parlando-style section (lines 39–45), the movement from shamisen, voice, and hayashi to instrumental interlude is repeated (cf. lines 1–20 and 39–47). A new combination is then heard (lines 48–51) because a new scene is portrayed, but the full ensemble sound soon returns to create an exciting finale. Though the tonal outline of Figure 22 is highly abstract, it does reflect an awareness that modulations to rarely heard pitches (such as C-sharp and G-sharp) enhance the sense of climax (lines 21–27 and 46–47). Rhythmic density, as implied by the changes in tempo, is yet another factor in the effectiveness of the overall structure of the composition.

Even this preliminary analysis of *Kanda matsuri* should be sufficient to convince one of the success of the composition. The work is all the more impressive when we recall that it is not the product of one person. As a communal composition, it is open to different orchestrations in different performances or recordings. The piece thus illustrates the maintenance of traditional compositional attitudes during a historical period when pressures to compose in a Western manner were strong. Despite this, "the composer" and his self-expression have been subsumed into a guild-created event.

If one were to continue to think in Western terms, a final question might be whether *Kanda matsuri* is a masterpiece. I don't think the question has ever been asked in that way by nagauta performers. At the time *Kanda matsuri* was written, it served its purpose well. Our preliminary analysis reveals that it has a mature internal structure, and the piece continues to be performed though its original historical reason for being has been forgotten. Perhaps this is the most important accolade. Though form follows function, the resulting product may serve more than its original purpose if it is powerful enough musically. *Kanda matsuri* is worthy of enjoyment and appreciation far beyond early-twentieth-century Japan and beyond the streets of Kanda.

FIFTH VIEW

Hōrai and the Art of Interpretation in Nagauta— One Composition in Four Performances

INTRODUCTION

Our previous views of Japanese music have already provided us with several insights into performance practice from a Japanese perspective. Perhaps the most important principle espoused so far has been the concept of relativity in relation to composition. By now it should be evident that one cannot view a traditional Japanese composition with the same absolutism with which one usually regards a Western classical piece such as a Beethoven symphony or a Mozart string quartet. In the West, considerable time and effort have been spent in recent decades searching for "authentic" renditions of such works. At the same time, there have been new performances of "classics" on the guitar, modern piano, or electronic synthesizer. In all of these cases, the original piece is always thought of as being totally the composer's work. In nagauta, however, we have already shown that composition tends to be a communal activity. We also noted that most performers are members of special guilds that assert their identity by the way they perform a given standard piece. A different combination of musicians may result in a discernibly different performance, though the same musicians performing the same piece are diligent in their accuracy and "correctness." We pointed out, moreover, that the "orchestration" of the hayashi parts in nagauta is as much a guild as a composer's activity.

Having been reminded of the concepts of accuracy and relativity in Japanese music, we are ready to study the challenging problem of interpretation. For this purpose we shall look at the nagauta composition *Hōrai*. It is chosen first because it is a lovely piece and second because it has been recorded several times. *Hōrai* also has the advantage of being a rather short "long song" (*nagauta*), lasting ten to eleven minutes. Thus it is more easily handled in comparative analyses. Finally, the style and origin of *Hōrai* give us views of nagauta that are different from those that we have seen so far. *Shakkyō* was a theater dance piece influenced by the noh drama, whereas *Kanda matsuri* was a concert piece with elements derived from urban festival music. *Hōrai* comes from a very different world.

HISTORY

The most unusual aspect of *Hōrai* historically is its origin. It apparently was written for a performance in celebration of the opening of a new geisha house in Edo (Tokyo).[1] Thus, as we compare performances, we might also be able to savor the distinctive flavors of shamisen music as it was served in Japan's famous floating world of the demimonde. Even historical data on *Hōrai* seem to belong to that hidden world. We do know that it was composed by Kineya Rokusaburō IV (1779?–1855), but we do not know the name of the lyricist, the date of the first performance, or the name of the geisha house where it occurred. It is dated vaguely between 1830 and 1844. The style of the text tempts one to guess that it might have been written by an employee or by the owner of the geisha house.[2]

TEXT

The text and translation of *Hōrai* are given below.[3] The names of formal divisions are rarely found in Japanese editions or commentaries. Those in parentheses have been added by me to facilitate comparisons between this piece and other nagauta compositions.

HŌRAI

Ni Agari
(*Maebiki, Oki, Michiyuki*)

1.	Uraraka na hi no iro somite	Steeped in brilliant sunlight,
2.	ko no ma ni mo	the flowers between the leaves of the trees
3.	hagoto no hana no ayanishiki	intermingle like the damask and brocade designs
4.	kasaneshi nui no date moyō	of a fine kimono.
5.	kitsutsu narenishi yamahime wa	Bedecked in such finery, the mountain princesses
6.	hito no nagame no mayoigusa	beguile men with their appearance.
7.	musubikanetaru soradoke wa	Their liaisons dissolve and are gone
8.	isso uwaki na soyokaze ya	like a capricious breeze.

(*Kudoki*)

9.	Uramite kemuru shiogama wa	Looking back at the smoking salt oven,
10.	mune ni taku hi no kiekanuru	an undying fire burning within,
11.	ē nan to shō	oh, what shall I do?
12.	adashi adanami	The fickle, flirting waves are welcomed,
13.	yosete wa kaesu iwamakura	then sent off, by the rocky pillow of the shore.
14.	ukina wa patto tatsu tori no	Scandal springs up suddenly, like a startled bird
15.	negura o shitō koi no yama	on the mountain where love yearns for a roost.

Honchōshi
(*Odori Ji*)

16.	Hagi no shiratsuyu	The white dew on the bush clover—
17.	oki fushi tsuraki	the luxuriant bed,
18.	iro to ka no shigerite fukaki	rich in color and perfume—
19.	toko no uchi	what a wretched existence!
20.	kesa no wakare ni	At morning's parting,

21.	sode nurasu shongae	a wetted sleeve. *Shongae.*
22.	Maneku susuki wa	The beckoning plume grass
23.	itazuramono yo	is but a mischievous rogue.
24.	ominaeshi aji na ki ni naru	The lady-flower so piquant,
25.	hana no iro	the bellflower
26.	samenu kikyō no	so charming—
27.	kawayurashi shongae	her color does not fade. *Shongae.*
28.	utsutsu na ya	It is as in a vision—

(*Chirashi*)

29.	Nagametsukisenu tonozukuri	One never tires of looking at the palace.
30.	ge ni Hōrai no miagureba	Truly, looking up at Mount Hōrai,
31.	takaki shirabe no matsugae ni	one hears among the pine boughs a high melody:
32.	koto hiku yō na	a crane, moving its feet

(*Dangire*)

| 33. | tsuru no ashidori | as if plucking a koto. |

A comparison of this text with our previous two texts should make it clear that we are in a different world indeed. Someone knowledgeable about Japanese literature will immediately note the many puns, double meanings, and innuendos in the text, and perhaps even the nonexpert can respond to the suggestiveness of the translation. It is not our purpose to study the text in detail, but a few comments are necessary if the reader is to understand the character of the words with which the composer and the performers have to work.

Though *Hōrai* is the name of a fabulous mythical mountain supposedly located in the sea between China and Japan, the term implies as well the brothel area of Edo.[4] The references to flowers throughout the poem are equally appropriate, for the original audience was filled with the "flowers" (*geisha*) of Edo. The use of the word *iro* (color) in the first line sets the geisha mood right away, for the word can mean lovemaking (see also lines 18 and 25). The description of the fine clothes of the nymphs on this fabulous mountain easily evokes the image of well-dressed geisha, who are sometimes known as mountain princesses. The evanescence of geisha-house love is obviously the topic of lines 7 and 8.

At first sight, the next line might seem odd, as it is an allusion to an old poem in the *Shin kokin wakashū*.[5] However, classical references occur in most Japanese texts. Here the heat of the salt ovens soon becomes the fire of love. Lines 12 and 13 take a jaundiced view of the waves of fickle customers who share a geisha's pillow. The word *adashi* can mean "fickle," "harmful," or "the enemy." Lines 14 and 15 reflect the complications of love in an environment best known to Westerners through the "floating world prints" (*ukiyoe*) that picture it. Scandal (*ukina*, "floating names") must surely have upset the beautiful birds of the brothel who so often dreamed of love.

The flowers listed in lines 16–27 are like the professional names of prostitutes, and may in fact have been the geisha flowers of the house for which *Hōrai* was composed. The reference to a luxuriant bed (*shigerite fukaki toko*) is obvious, but it should also be noted that the verb "to luxuriate" (*shigeru*) in geisha terms means "to sleep together." The wetted sleeve of line 21 has been a common motif for departing Japanese lovers for centuries. *Shongae* is not translated as it is a vocable that, like the English *fa la*, might be used to complete a line or verse. As suggested earlier, lines 22–27 may be an advertisement for the offerings of the house. The final verse once again plays on the implications of the name *Hōrai*. The references to koto music are properly evocative of sounds that one might hear in one of the better geisha houses, and the crane of line 32 is a common figure in images of the mythical mountain Hōrai as well as a symbol of good fortune.

We do not know what was the fate of that nineteenth-century geisha house or of its flowers and nymphs. However, the nagauta composition has moved on to the bourgeois recital world, and it is in recordings from that less evanescent setting that we shall find our musical flowers to pluck and appreciate.

SONIC SOURCES

Recordings are our best source of data on interpretation because the performances can be repeated without change and compared. The first two of the four record releases used in this study were chosen because they use the same singer but different shamisen accompaniments. The third was chosen because it is by a different school and different singers but uses one of the shamisen on the second recording. The fourth was chosen because it uses a female singer and yet other shamisen. The recordings of *Hōrai* will be identified by roman numerals, as follows:

I   = Columbia CL-18 (1955), side 2[6]
II   = Columbia CLS 5060 (1967), side 1, band 1
III = Crown LA 4054 (1967), side 2
IV   = Victor SJL 2220 (1966), side 2, band 2[7]

The names of the performers in these recordings are listed in Figure 23. Each performer is given an arabic number to assist us in the comparisons that follow. The singers, shamisen, and flutes are numbered in order from left to right, and the numbers for drummers and assistants are assigned primarily on the basis of guild affiliation.

A study of this list can teach us much about the hidden, sociohistorical world of Japanese music. We shall start at the bottom of the list, for only recordings I and II use assistants to play extra percussion instruments such as bells. Under the traditional system, all professional musicians must belong to some guild, and, as names 29 and 30 reveal, this is true even for assistants. These two names also show us that stage names must include the guild name and at least one syllable of the name of one's teacher. This principle can be seen further by comparing 16, 19, 20, and 21; 17, 18, and 22; 23 and 24; 26 and 27; and 6 and 7. The fact that the romanizations of the personal names of 19 and 26 and of 20 and 27 are the same is fortuitous, for they are written with different Chinese characters.

From the list of drummers we can see the dominance of the Mochizuki school in the recording business (16–22). Though performers 25–28 are from other schools, they are known individually for their work in dance and music recitals but not in kabuki performances. Thus they "belong" to the recording world, as most records are made for sale to persons in the dance and recital market.

Recording III is by the newest school, the Tōon kai. This group was founded in 1958 by Yamada Shōtarō (1899–1970) with students from the Tokyo University of Fine Arts. Its fresh, postwar di-

Recording

	I	II	III	IV
Singers	Yoshimura Ijūrō (1)	Yoshimura Ijūrō (1)	Miyata Tsuneo (3)	Kineya Satoyo (5)
		Imafuji Chōsuke (2)	Minagawa Ken (4)	
Shamisen	Kineya Eizō (6)	Yamada Shōtarō (8)	Kikuoka Hiroaki (9)	Imafuji Fumiko (11)
	Kineya Einosuke (7)	Kikuoka Hiroaki (9)	Kineya Yasaburō (10)	Imafuji Iyako (12)
Flutes	Fukuhara Eiji (13)	Fukuhara Hyakunotsuke (14)	Fukuhara Hyakunotsuke (14)	Fukuhara Hyakunotsuke (14)
				Hosei Haruo (15)
Drums	Mochizuki Kishisaburō (16)	Mochizuki Kishisaburō (16)	Mochizuki Sakichi (21)	Mochizuki Sakichi (21)
	Mochizuki Taijirō (17)	Mochizuki Tainosuke (18)	Mochizuki Taieimon (22)	Fukuhara Eiji (13)
	Tanaka Denjirō (25)	Mochizuki Kishirō (19)	Tosha Rōsetsu (23)	
	Katada Kishirō (26)	Mochizuki Kisaku (20)	Tosha Rōkei (24)	
		Katada Kisaku (27)		
		Uminoya Fukutarō (28)		
Assistant	Takeshiba Kaninosuke (29)	Takeshiba Munetsuke (30)		

Figure 23. *Hōrai* recording personnel.

rections are evident in the fact that it may use male and female performers in the same piece, and does *not* assign professional names.[8]
The drummers that it uses still live in the guild tradition, but note
that a different school is represented (23, 24). Recording IV combines a Mochizuki drummer (21) with a drummer heard in recording
I as a flute player (13). Note that the Fukuhara guild dominates the
flute business (13, 14); the performer not of that guild (15) is well
known not only as a nagauta flautist but also under his family name
of Wakayama as the head of a festival guild that we studied in the
Second and Fourth Views.

The intricacies of the guild system become even more complex
when we study the names of the shamisenists and singers of our recordings. Yoshimura Ijurō (b. 1901) and Kineya Eizō (b. 1890) are
both well known as kabuki and as concert musicians, and both were
active in the early-twentieth-century nagauta Kenkyū kai (music
study group) and the Kensei kai school that played important roles
in the development of concert nagauta.[9] Eizō[10] is of particular value
to us, as he wrote a series of commentaries on nagauta performance
practice, including remarks on the performance of *Hōrai*.[11] Thus we
have both his recorded performance and his written words on interpretation. Looking at the personal name of performer 7 in Figure 23,
one can tell that he belongs to Eizō's school. What is not evident is
that the Imafuji school of singer 2 grew out of Eizō's branch of the
Kineya genealogy.[12]

Before the dropping of professional names by the Tōon kai members (recording III), Yamada (8) also had a Kineya name, as did his
student Kikuoka (9), but their Kineya teacher was from a different
branch of this very large family tree. If one traces 6 and 8 genealogically back to the nineteenth century, both would meet at the tenth
Kineya Rokuzaemon (1800–1859) but separate at the eleventh and
twelfth. The main mentor of 8 and 9 was the second Kineya Jōkan
(1874–1956), who first had the name of Kineya Rokushirō, which
placed him in the genealogy of the Rokusaburō branch of the guild.[13]
Four generations *earlier*, in the late eighteenth century, the first Kineya Sakichi branched off from this group to form his own school,
which six generations *later* produced Kineya Satoyo (5), the singer of
our fourth recording. Her shamisen (11, 12) can be seen to be guild-
related to singer 2, whose school was shown to have branched off

from the group to which 6 belongs. Singers 3 and 4 were students of 9, who was a student of 8, so they, too, have roots in the Kineya genealogy.

What is the purpose of this peripatetic genealogical prelude to a study in interpretation? It is meant to make us aware of the strength of the common roots that support the entire structure of traditional Japanese arts. The great number of splits and new schools with related or new names sometimes reflect political or economic[14] moves by strong personalities, but often such new branches or schools seek to identify their differences in musical terms as well. Let us study the performances of *Hōrai* with the guild system as a constant, if hidden, background.

PERFORMANCE PRACTICE

The reader of earlier chapters will know that one aspect of nagauta performance practice is orchestration. Figure 24 shows how instruments are used in the four recordings. The orchestrations appear to be the same except for the second, third, and final sections. However, we should note that an obbligato second shamisen part is added to recording III, which greatly changes the color of the music, particularly in the opening maebiki section.

The orchestrations accompanying lines 1–8 are the most varied. The drums play in noh style in all four recordings; the differences in the patterns that they play will be discussed later. Whereas recording I supports the solo voice with only a bamboo flute and the tsuzumi drums, recording II enriches that accompaniment with the light sound of bells (*orugōru*). This sound is often associated with lyrical female dances and so is in keeping with the geisha spirit of the composition and the words at this point. Recording III is the only one to use the full hayashi plus the bells. Recording IV uses tsuzumi but adds a somewhat mysterious aura by having the noh flute enter with long tones in lines 3–4 and 6–7.[15]

On paper, the accompaniments of the odori ji look alike, but the actual uses of the bamboo flute are rather different. It plays gentle ornamentations of the shamisen line throughout this section in recording I, but tends to drop out in recordings II and III for the opening words of each line and for the big vocal solos on the word *shongae*

Recordings

Section	Text lines	I	II	III	IV
Maebiki		s	s	s	s
Oki, michiyuki	1–8 9	s + o + k + TB s	s + o + k + TB + B s	s + o + k + NK + T + B s	s + o + k + NK s
Kudoki	10–15	s	s	s	s
Odori ji	16–27 28	s + TB s	s + TB s	s + TB s	s + TB s
Chirashi	29–30 31–32	s + o + k s	s + o + k s	s + o + k s	s + o + k s
Dangire	33	s + o + k + TB	s + O + k + TB	s + o + k + T + NK	s + o + k + NK

Figure 24. *Hōrai* orchestrations. S = shamisen, O = ō tsuzumi, K = ko tsuzumi, TB = takebue (bamboo flute), NK = nōkan, T = taiko, B = bells.

so as not to interfere with the singer's musical highlights. In recordings III and IV the flute part is generally reduced to long-note abstractions of the basic pitches of the melody.

The final cadences of recordings I, II, and IV are very similar except for the use of a noh flute in recording IV, whereas recording III provides a fuller finale by the addition of a taiko along with a noh flute. In all, the orchestrations of these four performances, though similar, produce perceptibly different instrumental sounds. To obtain a complete view of this aspect of the tonal picture, see Figure 25, which shows the distribution of singers on the two recordings that are not rendered soloistically. Kineya Eizō, commenting in 1932 (p. 70), said that *Hōrai* can be used as a showpiece for a solo

	Recording II		Recording III	
Section	Text Lines	Singer	Text Lines	Singer
Oki, michiyuki	1–2	1	1–4	3
	3–4	1 + 2		
	5–6	2	5–8	4
	7–8	1	9	3
Kudoki	9–11	1	10–11	3
	12–15	2	12–15	3 + 4
Odori ji	16–19	1	16–21	3
	20–21	2		
	shongae	1		
	22–25	1	22–28	4
	26–27	2		
	shongae	1		
	28	1 + 2		
Chirashi	29–32	1 + 2	29–32	3 + 4
Dangire	33	1 + 2	33	3 + 4

Figure 25. The distribution of singers in *Hōrai*.

singer. He also noted that in his oldest copy of the piece three singers are listed (from the Okayasu guild), though he felt that using that many singers was going out of fashion.[16] He recommended the use of two singers so that the voice can be kept fresh, the instrumental interludes of *Hōrai* being rather short. Recordings II and III have followed his suggestion. However, the assigning of passages to singers 1 and 2 and their use together are strikingly different, as shown in Figure 25. Given the soloistic nature of *Hōrai*, modern printed notation of it gives no indications of who is to sing when. While such markings are found in many other notations of nagauta pieces, they are not followed rigidly.

What is to be learned about interpretation from Figure 25? The answer might be, the power of form and of prestige. The use of both singers for the final sections of both recordings seems quite natural. Their use in recording II for lines 3–4 may be related to the fact that the lines are part of the michiyuki, a section that traditionally uses a fuller texture. The thicker texture in recording III for lines 12–15 provides a sense that a section is ending, and creates a nice contrast to the tone color of the very popular odori ji of this piece. The handling of the odori ji in recording II seems to reflect the fame of Yoshimura, for he is given not only more lines but also the melismatic passages for the word *shongae* in both verses.

None of these differences is striking by itself, but when combined with the instrumentation as indicated in Figure 24, they do support the concept of relativity within a restricted framework that has been so basic to all our views of nagauta so far. Our present view will be enriched if we turn now to analysis of the actual music of *Hōrai*.

THE MAEBIKI

Example 25 * is a comparative score of the maebiki, the instrumental prelude to the oki, as it is performed on the four recordings. The obbligato shamisen part in recording III is not included. Suffice to say that it generally plays an octave higher than the melody and includes ornamenting pitches in some of the passages composed basically of quarter notes. The only instructions for the maebiki in the actual shamisen notation are the terms *kiwamete shizuka ni* (extremely quiet). Asakawa Gyokuto states in his commentaries that

Example 25. A comparative score of the maebiki of *Hōrai* (cassette example AA).

the opening of *Hōrai* should be smooth and relaxed (p. 125), and that the entire section in the ni agari tuning (i.e., through line 15) should be quiet and refined. Kineya Eizō, the shamisen player of recording I, says in his book that the opening should be tranquil (p. 64). A look at the tempo marking for recording I in Example 25 will tell us what he means by that in musical terms.[17] The tempo of recordings II and III might be explained by the fact that they are identified as dance-accompaniment recordings. However, recording IV and the second release of recording I (see n. 6) are also so identified.[18]

Eizō recalls (p. 64) that a disciple of his mother had said that this piece was in the style of *hauta*, a genre popular in geisha houses. This comment does not explain Eizō's exceptionally slow tempo, but it may account for certain aspects of the very different shamisen style of this opening, such as the glissandi in measures 1 and 14 and the stopped tones in measures 4, 6, 8, 14, and 17. These are not common in nagauta, but they are characteristic of geisha-house genres. However, Eizō's extensive use of these techniques may be more than an attempt to maintain the mood of the prelude; it may also be a method of giving the line a lyricism at this slow tempo. In this respect, Eizō's interpretation reminds me of a performance by a professional pianist of a lento movement by Mozart or Haydn. One need get maximum effect from minimum material. Note that the only other use of the stopped tone is in measure 14 of the next-slowest performance, recording IV. The tempo of recordings II and III does not accommodate such a gesture, though recording III does attempt this style in measure 11. Its change of pitch in measure 15 is related to the presence of an obbligato shamisen in this performance. In all the recordings a demimonde flavor is evoked by a tendency to play idiomatic eighth-note groups in the style crudely indicated in the transcription of measure 7 in recording IV. All the performers slow down in the last measures and place a space (a ma) before measure 20 in preparation for the first vocal entrance.

THE OKI AND MICHIYUKI

The oki and michiyuki of this piece seem to be combined into one section, for the first vocal and first hayashi entrances are very close. This unusual contraction of the form may be due to the length of the

instrumental prelude (maebiki) and the fact that the original performance was not on a stage that had a long entrance ramp. Example
26* is a comparative score of the vocal entrances as performed on the
four recordings. Yoshimura's recordings (I and II) differ only in the
ornamentation of measure 21 and in the speed with which the melody returns to B. In the Interlude we noted that vocal notation in
nagauta is deliberately vague with respect to rhythm and ornamentation. The slower tempo of recording I may help to account for its
more involved style. Concerning the vocal entrance, Eizō remarks in
his commentary (p. 65) that after the shamisen *shan* (the mnemonics
for the double stop in m. 20) the singer must draw a breath for a
moment before singing. He says that such "pulling sounds" (*hikine*)
are important in other types of music such as that of the taiko, as
well as in the famous comic dialogues of the *rakugo* genre.

   The reader may recognize in this last statement the concept of
space (ma) as an essential element in performance. It also relates to
another important concept called *koshi*. The word means the lower-
back or pelvic region of the body, and in the arts refers to a centering
of power in this area before performing an action such as singing or

Example 26. A comparative score of the first vocal passage in *Hōrai* (cassette example BB).

playing a phrase. It can be applied equally to a brush stroke in painting or a movement in the martial arts. From observations I feel that
it is often applied to everyday work activities as well.[19] In terms of
Japanese music, koshi could be one of our hidden views, for one does
not read about it, nor is it often mentioned in lessons. It is usually
learned from performance experience within a tradition over an extended period of time.

The vocal entrances in recordings III and IV seem less subtle than
those in recordings I and II, though the transcriptions do not ade-
quately represent the sonic events. Recall, however, that both these
recordings were made as dance accompaniment and thus may have a
greater need for a clear indication of important first beats. Nevertheless, they both exploit their own senses of nuance. The young
male singer in recording III is more elaborate in his ornamentation,
whereas the female singer's line looks rather bland in notation. What
is missing in the transcription is her use of a wide vibrato, which
would cloud any extensive melismas. Another, more obvious difference in interpretation is her entrance on the upper leading tone to B
rather than the lower, as in the other performances. I am tempted to
call this a more sensual entrance, but am not sufficiently familiar
with geisha music to speak with authority on this matter.

Eizō makes a remark about the shamisen music of measures 19–
20 that reflects yet another aspect of the nuances of nagauta interpretation. Using shamisen mnemonics, he says that to play these
three sounds *chi te to* is colorless; it is important that they be *chin ten
ton* (p. 65). What does this mean? Perhaps one will understand if one
looks back at the comments made on drum tone in the First View
(see p. 9). Apparently the length and closing of a tone are as important in shamisen playing as in drumming. Of course, nuance is a
most important hidden (i.e., unnotated) aspect of nearly all of the
world's art musics. Eizō's rare comments are of great help to us in dis-
covering similar sensitivities in the performance of Japanese music.

Example 27*, a comparative score showing the hayashi music at
the beginning of the michiyuki, brings another important element
into our study of interpretation. Figure 24 has already shown us that
the instrumentation varies: the bamboo flute appears in recordings I
and II and the noh flute in recordings III and IV, while bells are

Example 27. A comparative score of the michiyuki of *Hōrai* (cassette example BB).

heard in recordings II and III, and the taiko is heard in recording III only. The shamisen and the two tsuzumi are common to all four recordings, so only their parts have been transcribed. The basic shamisen line and the text are shown above and the four tsuzumi interpretations below. In all performances, the tsuzumi enter with some variant of the mitsuji pattern. The numbers in parentheses show, however, that a different beat 1 is used for each recording. The hayashi instruments thus seem to function as color rather than as specific

support for the melodic line. They are able to perform with this flexibility because their internal structure is secure though their rela-
tionships to the shamisen line may be very different in each performance. Adjustments need be made only when the final cadence of
the section appears. Example 27 certainly supports the sliding-doors
concept espoused in this study. However, the intellectual and structural power of the example is softened by the lyrical emphasis of the
vocal and shamisen lines of the piece.

Example 28 returns us to the shamisen part, here accompanying
the words *hana no ayanishiki* in line 3. Example 28a is a transcription
of the passage as it appears in shamisen notation. The mnemonics of
the notation for the pitches accompanying *a-ya* are *chin chin ten*, but
in Eizō's book they are *chin ten chin* (p. 65). He also gives special attention to the fingerings (third finger, open string, first finger) and
indicates which pitch should be sounded with which syllable. Example 28b is taken from recording I, in which Eizō performs. Note
that the two pitches in measure 5 have been reversed. The question is
why. The answer may be implied in a further remark by Eizō that the
measure is often played pizzicato in a geisha-house style that he does
not care for. By reversing the pitches, he has removed from his own
students the temptation to use that articulation. In the Yamada recording (II) the passage is played as notated in Example 28a, except
that the B in measure 5 is deleted. The same course is followed in
recording III, done by students of Yamada, whereas in recording IV
the passage is played exactly as notated in Example 28a.

Eizō says that the passage should be played smoothly (*sura sura*),
and Asakawa remarks (p. 125) that the entire section in the ni agari
tuning (through line 15) requires a long, smooth style of singing.
Perhaps Asakawa's most significant statement is that one should interpret the lines freely in order not to make them boring. With that

Example 28. Two versions of one shamisen passage in *Hōrai*.

Example 29. Four vocal renditions of "hito no nagame no" in *Hōrai* (cassette example CC).

in mind we turn in Example 29* to the vocal rendition of line 6. Though recordings I and II are by the same singer, the difference in the point of entry should not be surprising in the light of earlier comments about the fluidity of solo vocal style. The contour of the vocal line on the word *nagame*, however, is noteworthy. Neither performance follows an admonition of Eizō that *ga* should be sung higher than *me* (p. 65). Perhaps Yoshimura was thinking of the eye (*me*) looking around (*nagameru*) at the beautiful sights of the Yoshiwara geisha-house district when he widened the contour of the line in both performances. Then again, he may simply have been following the contour of the printed notation, which places *na* on B, *ga* on C-sharp, and *me* on F-sharp. Miyata on recording III generally stays closer to the shamisen line, but uses the F-sharp on *me* also.[20] It is our female singer on recording IV who follows Eizō's wishes most closely. Perhaps this reflects her training in the Kineya guild from which her professional name is derived. However, her vibrato and heterophonic extensions of the word seem more "feminine" (i.e., geisha) in style.

Before leaving this section we should note that none of the commentaries by Eizō and Asakawa mentions any hayashi part, though hayashi sounds are present on the recordings as we saw in Figure 24.

This can be accounted for by the compositional practice noted in the Interlude (p. 49) and by the fact that the commentaries were written for voice and shamisen students. In all our performances the hayashi drops out after line 8, and by line 9 the thinner, lyrical texture of a kudoki is established.

THE KUDOKI

The removal of the hayashi and use of the standard *tataki* shamisen style (cf. Example 22) are typical characteristics of kudoki lyricism. Tataki-like accompaniments appear on F-sharp for line 10 and on D for line 12. Asakawa emphasizes the vocal importance of this section by saying that there is a need for a gradual change to a brighter (*hade*) style (p. 126). Example 30* is a comparative score of the most sensual passage, the setting of line 11, for the words are a geisha's expression of "Oh, what shall I do?" Note first the shamisen slides and the sudden use of C-sharp with its miyako-tetrachord–geisha-music implication. Though the shamisen notation shows measure 5 in a usual 2/4 length, all the singers use more time as they elaborate on the first syllable of the word *nan* (what). Here the interpretations clearly differ. Yoshimura emphasizes the final *n* in both recordings (I and II) to give the passage a romantic humming vocalise before the open sounds of *to* and *shō*. Kineya Satoyo (recording IV) lets the *a* ring out first with an upper-leading-tone ornament and maintains her usual delayed-cadence style. Miyata (recording III) opts for a vocalise on *to*. In short, our few comparative scores show that while vocal lines are relative, they are based on a personal sense of style and interpretation.

The renderings of line 14 offer us yet further treasures of interpretation. The word *patto* is rather like the English word *pop* and so has onomatopoeic possibilities, and the analogy with startled birds is clearly open to musical imitation. Example 31* shows the notated shamisen line for this passage along with the text. All the singers make a sharp break between the two syllables of *patto*. In recording I, Yoshimura places a brief ornament on the second syllable, as does Imafuji in recording II. Since two singers are performing *patto* in recording III, the second syllable is given no special treatment. In recording IV the last syllable is spoken rather than sung. The hopping of the startled birds has an obvious influence on the shamisen accompaniment in measure 5–8. Its interpretation in recording I, however, is quite different from that in the other recordings. The tempo is already somewhat slower than in the other performances, so there is time to play the first two pitches of measure 5 staccato and with a slight allargando. Thereafter, all performances move in a flexible tempo that is a standard signal that the end of this section of a composition has been reached.

Example 30. Four versions of "ē nan to shō" in *Hōrai* (cassette example DD).

uki — na   wa   pat' to   ta–tsu   tori   no ——

Example 31. Word painting in *Hōrai* (cassette example EE).

THE ODORI JI

The change of shamisen tuning to honchōshi (a fourth and a fifth) is a normal indication of a new section in nagauta compositions. Eizō mentions (p. 67) that the style of this section is inspired by an early popular genre called *hinda odori*. This term is found in two of the earliest publications of shamisen music as part of the *kumiuta* tradition: the Ōnusa volume of the *Shichiku taizen* (1686) and the *Matsu no ha* (1703).[21] The hinda odori have survived in folk forms,[22] as well as in other nagauta compositions such as *Utsubozaru* (discussed by Eizō on pp. 130–31). If one compares all these pieces, there seems to be no thematic relation between the nagauta version of this genre and the surviving performances of the hinda odori in folk and kumiuta music. However, the use of a strophic form, a shamisen ostinato, a pentatonic tonality, and a wide-range vocal entrance in the odori ji of *Hōrai* seems inspired by the earlier popular or folk music styles.

A comparative score of the shamisen prelude to the first verse is shown in Example 32*. The tempo differences are not unlike those noted at the beginning of the opening prelude of the piece (cf. Example 25). Tonally, the basic emphasis in this prelude and the strophs that follow is on the pentatonic (yonanuki) scale common to folk and popular idioms. Note that Yamada and his disciples (recordings II and III) follow the notated version of the piece in measure 7 in the use of F-natural, whereas Kineya Eizō and the genealogically related Imafujis (recordings I and IV) prefer to maintain the original tonal image. Another distinction between these two sets of interpretations is the greater use of geisha-music "offbeat" accents in measures 5 and 9 in recordings II and III.[23] Recordings I and IV take an opposite approach in measure 9. Recording I, being slower, is able to add more stopped tones (mm. 2 and 9) and use a slide in lieu of the dotted rhythm in measure 3, whereas recording IV reduces the final

pitch of that measure to a nearly inaudible grace note. (Recording IV
also changes m. 8.) Recording IV uses slides to achieve a romantic
lyricism, whereas recording I reduces the number of accents to create
a slow, flowing line on a plucked instrument. This is consistent with

Example 32. A comparative score of the opening of the odori ji in *Hōrai* (cassette
example FF).

Kineya's comment (p. 67) that this entire section of *Hōrai* became popular as a separate piece, particularly among geisha, who sometimes performed it so stylishly (*ikisugi*) that it sounded more like kiyomoto than nagauta.[24] This change of style is evident in all the recordings, for the shamisen play more lightly than usual in nagauta and thus produce a thinner tone more characteristic of that of the kiyomoto shamisen.

To the shamisen line we need now add the vocal part. The first obvious observation concerning the vocal part has to do with the length of the first phrase. As seen after measure 13 in Example 32, Yoshimura holds his F-sharp one measure longer than the other singers. Such a difference in performance is well known to Eizō, as is evident in the following anecdote:

> Once I attended a practice session and played *Hōrai* with one singer. The singer was a geisha of that neighborhood and her singing was fairly good. Up until *koi no yama* I played very comfortably. However, when we got to the *honchōshi* section I played *te re ton* [B B E] several times before the singer came in with *hagi no*. Her pitch raised there and did not come down, so I had to play *te re ton* so many times I could not count them. When she finally came to the ending word *shongae* the verse had been so changed that I did not know where to play the cadence. At that point things were like muddy tea and, although it was winter, I perspired a lot. (p. 68)

Example 33* shows the degree to which the final passage mentioned in Eizō's anecdote is open to various interpretations. As the first two recordings are so similar they are presented as one version though the keen listener will hear differences in cassette example GG. Recordings III and IV both shorten the vocalise on *n* by two beats and remain consistent in their styles, recording III adhering the closest to the beat and pitches of the shamisen line. The free style of recording IV in measure 8 may have influenced the shamisen, who play an F-natural in measure 9 that is quite out of keeping with the pentatonic core of this section. It could be a sign of confusion, or a deliberate geishalike "blues" note for this moment in the piece. The shamisen also drop one beat from measure 12. This may be related to the choreography of the dancers who use Kineya Satoyo's recordings. These final vocalise variants help to explain Eizō's comments and his sweat.

Example 33. A comparative score of "shongae" in *Hōrai* (cassette example GG).

In our excerpts from the odori ji we have seen several tempi and interpretations. How, then, is one to decide how to perform this section? Asakawa says that one should study the performances of several great musicians before arriving at one's own interpretation (p. 126). He cautions the shamisen to be aware of its role here as accompaniment to the vocal line. He suspects a *kouta* genre influence, but also leaves room for a more lively folk-song style (*jinku*). Perhaps the most interesting comment that he makes concerns the strophic structure of this section. Recall that nagauta in general is through-composed and is not strophic except when it is imitating folk or popular music. For Asakawa, this musical redundancy does not mean that one ignores the text. Apparently reflecting on performances that he has heard, he comments that while the first verse (lines 16–21) is usually performed conventionally (*mongiri*), the second (lines 22–27) can be done in a different mood by singing it more theatrically (*keren*, "playing to the gallery"). I do not note this difference in the recordings of this study, but a look at the vocal excerpts in Examples 32 and 33 shows how such differences are possible.

If we study all our transcriptions of vocal sections in the piece, we can see three aurally distinct vocal styles. The consistency of Yoshimura's style is evident in those passages in which his colleague (Imafuji) is singing (Examples 30 and 32); his own flexibility is evident in moments like that shown in Example 29. The Tōon kai singers (recording III) seem to prefer a less ornamented style, adhering more closely to the line of their shamisen-playing leader. Our female interpreter has developed a very different style, with a broader vibrato and ornamentation and a preference for later entrances of cadence tones. We have noted further that the shamisen players have gone to great pains to produce either lyrical or lively lines according to their own preferences or in response to the needs of the singers.

At this point the compelling question for many Western musicians may be, Which interpretation is correct? Those who have followed our previous views of Japanese music should have the answer. Speaking in terms of the odori ji only, I see the mood of the words as calling for the slower tempo, but this may reflect more on the interpreter than on the music. If the line is played faster, the music is more folklike and less romantic. The text seems to call for romance, but if it is read as an advertisement of the best the house has to offer perhaps a brighter rendition is in order. Thus, to judge an interpretation of this section of *Hōrai*, perhaps one has to ask first another question: What kind of geisha do you want to visualize?

As I meditate on this interpretive problem, an image comes to mind from a very different tradition. It is the view of a fine noh mask. As one watches a masked actor move about on a noh stage and as the dramatic situation changes, often the expression on the mask really seems to change as well. Is it the angles of one's view, the effect of the music and drama, or a change in the insight of the viewer? It all seems relative. Such a flexible view is essential, for without it one may be like a tourist who looks at and buys postcard pictures but never sees the real beauties of the area.

THE CHIRASHI AND DANGIRE

Line 28 is sung as a cadence, but its text forms a bridge between the odori ji and the final section. In performances the texture for lines 29–32 becomes denser in a typical chirashi manner. In the recordings, the tsuzumi play kabuki style (chiri kara) while the singers give out text in a straightforward syllabic manner. Example 34* shows the one moment in which there is an obvious relation between the music and the text. The plucking (*hiku*) of the koto is clearly imitated by the shamisen. The crane, as a standard Japanese symbol of good fortune, stands most appropriately in the text of the dangire final cadence. In the first performance of *Hōrai* such symbolism was

Example 34. Word painting in *Hōrai* (cassette example HH).

meant to augur well for the new house for which the piece was composed. We do not know the fate of that establishment, or of the
feminine flowers that bloomed or withered within it. We do know
that the composition has remained popular for over one hundred
years. Perhaps our study of this piece has helped us to appreciate not
only the performance possibilities of the piece but also the seriousness with which the better musicians of Japan approach the hidden
art of interpretation.

The Noh Play *Sumidagawa* and Benjamin Britten's *Curlew River*—One Story in Two Musical Worlds

NOH DRAMA AND BENJAMIN BRITTEN

An introduction to the noh drama with special attention to its musical elements was given in the Interlude. Studies of the impact of this form of music drama on Western theater are also available in European-language materials.[1] Of particular interest to us in this study is the attempt of symbolist playwrights such as Yeats to incorporate aspects of noh into Western drama.[2] Because of these efforts, Benjamin Britten's first exposure to a live performance of noh was probably conditioned by previous intellectual experience in the goals of such Western theater. Nevertheless, his comments on this occasion indicate his surprise and inspiration:

> It was in Tokyo in January 1956 that I saw a Nō-drama for the first time: and I was lucky enough during my brief stay there to see two different performances of the same play—Sumidagawa. The whole occasion made a tremendous impression upon me: the simple, touching story, the economy of style, the intense slowness of the action, the marvellous skill and control of the performers, the beautiful costumes, the mixture of chanting, speech, singing, which, with the three instruments, made up the strange music—it all offered a totally new "operatic" experience.
>
> There was no conductor—the instrumentalists sat on the stage, as did the chorus, and the chief characters made their entrance down a long ramp. The lighting was strictly nontheatrical. The cast was all male, the one female character wearing an exquisite mask which made no attempt to hide the male jowl beneath it.
>
> The memory of this play has seldom left my mind in the years since. Was there not something—many things—to be learnt from it? The solemn dedication and skill of the performers were a lesson to any singer or actor of any country and any language. Was it not possible to use just such a story—the simple one of a demented mother seeking her lost child—with an English background (for there was no question in any case of a pastiche from the ancient Japanese)? Surely the Medieval Religious Drama in England would have had a comparable setting—an all-male cast of ecclesiastics—a simple austere staging in a church—a very limited instrumental accompaniment—a moral story? And so we came from Sumidagawa to Curlew River and a Church in the Fens, but with the same story and similar characters: and whereas in Tokyo the music was the ancient Japanese music jealously preserved by successive generations, here I have started the work with that wonderful plainsong hymn "Te lucis ante terminum," and from it the whole piece may be said to have grown. There is nothing specifically Japanese left in the Parable that William Plomer and I have written, but if stage and audience can achieve half the intensity and concentration of that original drama I shall be well satisfied.[3]

This, then, was the challenge that England's best operatic composer chose to accept. The work *Curlew River* was completed in Vienna in 1964 and premiered at Orford Church, Suffolk, on June 12, 1964, as part of the Aldeburgh Festival. I had the pleasure of seeing the Caramoor Festival Company production of it at the Fairland Festival in Dearborn, Michigan, on July 5, 1967. I was already familiar with the noh and kabuki versions of the story. I found the work unique not only in terms of Britten's other compositions but also in its ability to capture the spirit of noh and to respond to its musical essence without direct imitation. The function of our final view is to describe the surface and hidden elements of the original noh play and compare them with the contents of Britten's work. This is done without any pretense of expertise on noh drama, opera, or the works of Benjamin Britten.[4] Rather, the present study is designed as a quite different illustration of the book's favorite principle: the world of music consists of a whole series of equally logical but different systems. This study may also help us to see how the two pieces are equally beautiful and capable of telling us as much about the cultures in which they were created as they do about their creators.

THE PRODUCTIONS

Certain aspects of the *Curlew River* production were simple to adapt from the noh drama. The most obvious one is the use of an all-male cast, as professional noh has always used men, though women may study noh and perform in amateur recitals. The all-male convention was easily met in *Curlew River*, for the parable play is done by a cast of monks. In noh, the main character (shite) wears a mask, but the secondary character (waki) and additional actors (*tsure* or *waki tsure*) do not. The woman, ferryman, and traveller in *Curlew River* wear eye masks or half masks with large eye openings and nothing obstructing the nose or mouth (see Figure 26). Such "practical" masks contrast with those of the noh, which cover most of the face and thus muffle the voice and limit the vision of the actor.[5] The last-named characteristic has a profound effect on the types of movements the main actor may execute.

In terms of costumes, little needs to be said except that those used in *Curlew River* are as appropriate to the period in which the opera is set as those used in *Sumidagawa* are to its time and caste. The clearest relation between the two productions is seen in their stagings. Figure 27a is a diagram of a traditional noh stage and Figure 27b a drawing of the original setting for *Curlew River*. To help the reader visualize the two productions we shall discuss a few features of these stages. In the noh theater, the entrance ramp (hashigakari) is in full view of the audience, and the main actor's first turn towards the audience traditionally occurs on this ramp just before he enters onto the actual stage. The hayashi and any stage assistants (*kōken*) sit across the back of the stage, and the chorus (ji), entering through a special side door, sit at a right angle to the hayashi along the side of the stage. The pillar at the point where the stage and the ramp meet is called the naming pillar or shite pillar, because it is the area in which characters identify themselves and where the shite is

Figure 26. The main characters in *Curlew River*. Photo by Reg Wilson.

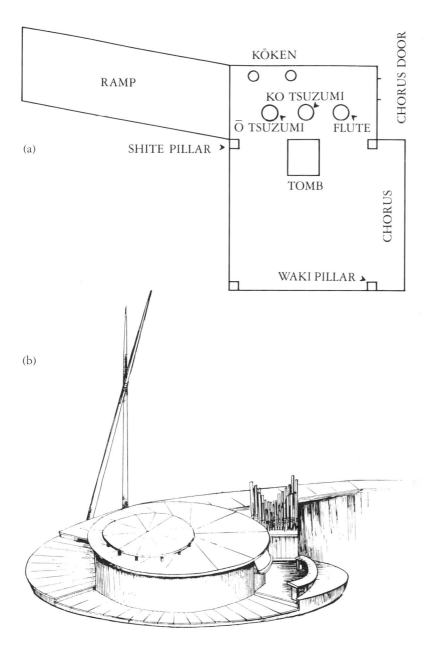

(a)

RAMP

KŌKEN

KO TSUZUMI

Ō TSUZUMI   FLUTE

CHORUS DOOR

SHITE PILLAR ►

TOMB

CHORUS

WAKI PILLAR ►

(b)

Figure 27. (a) The noh stage. (b) The *Curlew River* stage. Reprinted, by permission, from Colin Graham, *Production Notes and Remarks on the Style of Performing "Curlew River"* (London: Faber & Faber, 1965), p. 2.

often placed during much of a play. Diagonally across from this pillar is the waki pillar, so called because the waki often sits or stands there.

As seen in Figure 27b, Colin Graham's setting for use in a church has an equally visible ramp and open stage. The instrumentalists are in full view on the lower level, above which a large main-stage circle and a smaller raised center circle are built for the action. One difference between the two stagings is that there are two props in *Curlew River*, which are changed, and in *Sumidagawa* there is only one (a mound), which is set onstage before the play begins.

The instrumentation of both plays is small and transparent. The noh uses only the flute and the two tsuzumi drums, as no traditional dance occurs in the play that requires the taiko. *Curlew River* uses a small organ, harp, double bass, horn, flute, and viola and percussion. In both cases, there is no conductor and the instrumentalists, singers, and chorus must receive cues from one another.

We turn now to stage action. The movements on a noh stage are much more restrained than those of *Curlew River*. (A kabuki production of the play is more active than either.) The noh tradition of named, stereotyped movements and gestures is matched in *Curlew River* by a special set of instructions printed with the score. Colin Graham's admonition is of particular interest:

> Involvement can be shattered by a single uncontrolled, weak, or unnecessary gesture. Every movement of the hand or tilt of the head should assume immense meaning and, although formalized, must be designed and executed with the utmost intensity: this requires enormous concentration on the part of the actor, an almost Yoga-like muscular, as well as physical, control.[6]

If we are to appreciate the goals of our two performances we must compare this twentieth-century statement with the writings of Zeami Motokiyo (1363–1444), one of the founders of noh. Zeami conceived of noh training as consisting of nine stages, the last three being called the flowers (*hana*) of tranquil equilibrium, innermost profundity, and mysterious singularity.[7] We cannot digress into all the philosophical implications of these categories, but quotations from Zeami's works may illuminate certain aspects of the works that we are studying. In the *Kadensho* [The flower-tradition writings], we find the following statement about the relation of body movement to music:

> The shite has to devise his movement according to the meaning of the words. . . . Using his body in this way to fit the meaning of every phrase is the very basis of his style.[8]

Since our main character is a woman, Zeami's remarks in *Shūgyoku tokka* [Collecting gems and obtaining flowers] are also germane:

> As for the pattern of impersonation of the female, I have named it "focusing on the mind and relinquishing physical strength" (*tai shin sha riki*). . . . Striving merely to imitate womanhood without having modeled oneself on this basic pattern could never lead to the actualization of the allotted caliber of woman. On the contrary, one's attitude of consciously striving to imitate womanhood itself disqualifies one from being woman.[9]

Later, he says:

> It is a rare accomplishment for a player to attain the fame of virtuosity by truly assimilating his inner self with the personage he is impersonating. This certainly would correspond to the Chinese saying "The difficulty exists not in achieving something but in achieving it with perfection."[10]

With these heady remarks by English and Japanese directors in mind, we can now move on to the two plays and their performances.

THE STORY

The noh drama *Sumidagawa* is attributed to Jūrō Motomasa (1395–1459), who was one of Zeami's sons. The libretto of *Curlew River* was written by William Plomer, who used an English translation of the noh play as a guide.[11] Both the translation and Plomer's text are available in English publications, and there are several annotated editions of the original Japanese text.[12] Therefore, instead of presenting a complete comparative text as in previous chapters, we shall start with a general plot summary and then move to more detailed discussions of the drama and its two versions, quoting text where necessary.

In the noh classification system, *Sumidagawa* is of the fourth general type, specifically a madwoman play. No legend or historical event has been found as a source for the story, but, unhappily, the plot could easily have been derived from current events of the period. The Sumida is a large river in Tokyo. At the time in which the piece was written, rivers were usually crossed by ferryboat or, if the river was shallow, by porter or sedan chair. The events of this play are said to occur in a country area that later became the Asakusa part of Edo,[13] a place better known to us as the sensual floating world through which we travelled in our previous views. Britten and Plomer situate their Curlew River in a similarly distant location for medieval England. It is the Fens marshlands in Lincolnshire (perhaps north of the English town called Boston). The noh play is set in spring on the fifteenth day of the third month. Its basic action is as follows.

A ferryman identifies the location and speaks of a memorial service that is to take place across the river. A traveller on his way from Kyoto (Miyako) to visit a friend describes his journey and then asks for passage on the ferry. The ferryman inquires about unusual sounds back along the road, and the traveller explains that a madwoman is dancing there. The ferry is held so that the madwoman can be observed. She arrives, speaking of a search for her son, who was kidnapped by a slaver. She asks for boat passage, but the ferryman wants her to dance first. They enter into an argument, for she is a former noblewoman from Kyoto and he is but a boatman. He identifies a bird by its everyday name, but she uses its poetic name, and as she calls for news of her child from the bird, the ferryman relents and lets her on board. As the boat crosses, the traveller asks about the people on the other shore, and, while poling, the ferryman tells the story of a young boy who was left there by a cruel foreigner a year before. The boy was dying and, after identifying himself, asked that he be buried by the road so that the shadows of passersby from Kyoto might touch his grave. The traveller decides to join the other people who now pray there. The woman asks for more details from the ferryman, and realizes that this was her son. She is led to the grave, where, in her grief, she asks for people to dig up the body so that she may see her son again. The ferryman gives the mother a small Buddhist gong and tells her to pray instead for the repose of her son's soul. The mother joins the other people in prayer. Then she begins to hear the voice of her son responding to the prayers. His ghost appears, but as she tries to touch it, the vision fades and she is left to weep alone.

To turn this powerful Buddhist story of the evanescence of life into a Christian medieval mystery parable, Britten and Plomer have added several elements, for example, a Gregorian hymn as a processional and recessional, and an abbot who opens and closes the play with sermonlike comments. The core of the original text, however, is handled with great respect. Words are added primarily to allow for more Western-style action. A Christian ending is constructed, for the child's prayers bring the mother out of her madness and into salvation.

We shall review the plot again as we proceed in our discussion. Let us begin by showing the formal structure of the noh play, for we can then use its terms as guideposts in the musical studies that follow.

THE FORM

The veteran traveller through the scenes of this book has perhaps already predicted that the texts of publications and performances of *Sumidagawa* are not always exactly the same. This is particularly true if different schools of noh are involved. Scholarly editions of the noh texts also do not always use the same larger divisions, though they are usually consistent in the use of the names of musical sections.[14] The formal outline given below combines such divisions and terms in a way that agrees with other references to noh form found earlier in this book. Brackets are used to indicate hayashi rather than vocal sections. Terms in parentheses are added by the author.

JO NO DAN

[nanoribue]	entrance of waki (ferryman)
nanori	waki monologue
[shidai]	entrance of tsure (traveller)
shidai	traveller's first travel song
nanori	traveller monologue
ageuta (michiyuki)	traveller's second travel song
mondō	dialogue about the boat and woman

HA NO MAEDAN

[issei]	entrance of shite (madwoman)
sashi and issei	poetry reference and madwoman's thoughts
[kakeri]	madwoman's dance
sashi	madwoman's story
sageuta and ageuta	choral extension of story

HA NO CHŪDAN

mondō	dialogue between woman and ferryman, including poetry quotations about birds
ageuta	choral extension of bird imagery
mondō	woman allowed on the boat
katari	ferryman's story of the boy
mondō	traveller's joining in praying, woman's realization that the grave is her son's

HA NO ATODAN

kudoki	mother's lament at the grave
sageuta and ageuta	choral extension of lament

KYŪ NO DAN

mondō	mother persuaded by ferryman to pray
(nembutsu)	prayer
uta (kiri)	appearance and disappearance of son's ghost

As a viable theatrical tradition, noh cannot be expected to follow the conventions of its form rigidly. At the same time, such through-composed works must proceed in such a manner that an informed listener senses a logical and inevitable forward motion. In the formal outline shown, we see that the tradition of dividing two-act plays into five dan has been applied to the one-act structure of *Sumidagawa*. The first dan is extended beyond the michiyuki to a mondō because the two secondary actors enter separately and the traditional description of a journey is assigned to the tsure. The entrance of the main actor in the second dan is done to hayashi accompaniment only; the convention of a first-act dance is observed in her dementia scene. The ageuta of the third dan provides further opportunities for choreographic power, and the fourth dan places a key dance in a proportionally correct position within the play. The last dan is not identified by the usual finale terms, as the Buddhist prayer (*nembutsu*) assumes an important role, and the ghost is a child (*kokata*) and a new actor instead of the main actor returning in a new guise as in standard two-act plays. The chorus's sad commentaries as the mother makes futile attempts to touch her son provide a powerful close to her last movements. The intensity of *Sumidagawa* builds in such an effective manner that its adaptation to Western theatrical media is rather easy, but the aesthetics of the two traditions are different.

THE MUSIC

With the names of the sections of noh drama as guides, we shall now seek to describe the obvious and hidden musical elements of *Sumidagawa* and *Curlew River*. Since a recording of *Curlew River* is commercially available,[15] the excerpts on the book cassette are entirely from *Sumidagawa*, as performed on a videotape purchased from the Japanese National Broadcasting Corporation (NHK).[16] Transcriptions from *Sumidagawa* are also derived from that source. To keep the music in its theatrical context, line drawings from the Kanze school songbook[17] (*utaibon*) and from the production notes of *Curlew River* have been incorporated into the text. Theatrical and musical events are difficult to evoke with printed words, but we hope that the final journey of this book will offer the reader views of similar artistic paths travelled by composers separated by some five hundred years.

THE JO NO DAN

Nanoribue

We have mentioned that Britten, in order to give *Curlew River* the flavor of a medieval mystery play, begins with a procession of monks. They sing the Gregorian hymn *Te lucis ante terminum*, the first verse of which says:

> Before the light has passed away,
> Dear Lord, we come in prayer to thee;
> Oh, be our guide, our guard, our stay,
> And soothe us with thy clemency.[18]

An abbot then addresses the congregation (audience) to prepare them for a story concerning God's grace. Drum punctuations and soft tone clusters on the organ produce an "exotic" timbre behind the abbot's speech, but Britten's structural goals remain true to his Western ideals throughout. First, there is the Western necessity for musical themes that are repeated or developed. Example 35 shows the opening phrase of the chant, the call and response of the abbot and the monks, and the instruments' entrance. This cadence (a drop of a

Example 35. A Gregorian hymn from *Curlew River*. Reprinted, by permission, from Benjamin Britten, *Curlew River* (London: Faber & Faber, 1965).

minor third) is found throughout the opera, particularly when prayer or God is involved.[19] The use of the same call and response and the same chant for the processional and recessional of the composition is a further example of that very Western need for the return and balance of musical material. It is *not* a need in Japanese music. This need is so powerful a force in much of Western music that we tend to take it for granted though we know that word-oriented, through-composed music was a part of Europe's medieval and Renaissance world.

The abbot's speech is followed by an instrumental interlude during which the monks who are to play roles in the play are ceremonially dressed in costume. This interlude lasts almost as long (ninety seconds) as the opening flute solo (nanoribue) that is used to accompany the entrance of the waki in *Sumidagawa*. Recall that Britten specifically stated that he had no interest in imitating the music of noh. Nevertheless, it is impressive how he did, in fact, capture the essence of such music in his own idiom, as is evident in this first moment of parallel activity in the two compositions. Example 36* is a transcription of the last phrase of the flute introduction in the noh, and Example 37 shows the notation of the opening of the last

Example 36. The nanoribue from *Sumidagawa* (cassette example II).

Example 37. A *Curlew River* instrumental interlude. Reprinted, by permission, from Benjamin Britten, *Curlew River* (London: Faber & Faber, 1965).

Example 38. The ferryman's motive in *Curlew River*. Reprinted, by permission, from Benjamin Britten, *Curlew River* (London: Faber & Faber, 1965).

period of Britten's instrumental interlude. The highly fluid linear style of the noh version is effectively matched, for all the instruments in Britten's passage are equally linear and their total sound is deliberately blurred by slight differences in rhythm or articulation. The harp, horn, and viola are particularly important in this respect. "Theme" arises in the chant-related cadence seen in Example 37. Of course, noh-flute melodies often consist of rearrangements of themes, that is, stereotyped units (see the Interlude, p. 44), but these melodies are drawn from the entire noh repertory rather than from one piece. This section in both pieces is designed to give the listener time to enter into the mood of the play through transparent textures, both of which are quite beautiful though different. It is during this section of *Sumidagawa* that the boatman enters.

Nanori

In the noh play the boatman, standing close to the first pillar, identifies himself, the place, and the people across the river. He speaks unaccompanied, in stylized speech (*kotoba*). Example 38 shows that Britten's ferryman is given an instrumental identifying mark: quick, conjunct movements on the French horn. The interjection of drumrolls may be noh-inspired, though its style is very much its own.[20]

Shidai

A hayashi interlude of some three minutes and forty-five seconds begins this section of *Sumidagawa*. The flute periods are widely spaced, and it is only on the flute's third entrance that the tsure appears on the ramp and moves to the first pillar on the stage.[21] Britten's traveller is already onstage, so the instrumental accompaniment of his movements is only some thirty seconds long. The significant theatrical-aesthetic difference between

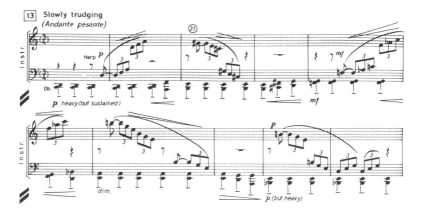

Example 39. The traveller's motive in *Curlew River*. Reprinted, by permission, from Benjamin Britten, *Curlew River* (London: Faber & Faber, 1965).

the two versions of this moment is in the use in *Sumidagawa* of a long period of hayashi music in which "nothing happens" onstage. It is moments like this that perhaps best demonstrate the differences between a Buddhist and a Christian methodology. Having entered the noh play, one is given time to meditate, to "center" without the distractions of action or text, while the hayashi clears one's mind of extraneous thought. When the tsure finally speaks ("To the far Eastland I am bound; Tedious days of travel lie before me"), he, like the waki, stands absolutely still without gesture. The drums continue behind his speech, and his last line is handled in a conventional noh manner by being repeated quietly by the chorus. Britten conforms to this tradition by using choral repetitions of selected words from the traveller's last two phrases. As seen in Example 39, the traveller's instrumental marker is an arpeggiated harp line accompanied in this section by a "walking" double bass. Note how skillfully it suppresses the harmonic implications by the conflict of the bass and harp lines. This is yet another important gesture towards the linear, non-Western ideal that Britten is seeking.

Nanori

In *Sumidagawa*, the traveller identifies himself in unaccompanied stylized speech. It is subtly different from that of the boatman heard earlier because he is of a different class. In *Curlew River*, the traveller's musical marker is heard throughout this section.

Ageuta (Michiyuki)

The drums return in *Sumidagawa* to accompany the  traveller as, without moving, he describes his journey. This text is sung in the strong (*tsuyo*), masculine style. The flute is heard in the next four lines of text, but note that it never plays the tsure's melody. The flute line is integrated with the drum parts, which in turn are integrated with the singing. It is this less obvious integration that hides the logic of the structure of noh music from many Western ears.

Only during these final lines does the traveller begin to move. He then returns to stylized speech, though the first line is accompanied by the ko tsuzumi so that the change in style is not abrupt.

In *Curlew River*, the motive of the arpeggiated harp and walking double bass carries the traveller through his journey. The vocal line responds to the Western need for drama by rising to its highest pitch some two-thirds of the way into the song, at "Many a peril I have faced." The line then uses the chant cadence as the traveller prays for protection. This quiet message may be the Christian equivalent of the meditations that we noted earlier in *Sumidagawa*. In *Curlew River* we now hear the French horn, marking the nearness of the boat landing and the ferryman.

Mondō

In *Sumidagawa*, unaccompanied stylized speech is used to set the scene of dialogue between the waki and the tsure, who stand rigidly in their proper places. The choral entrance at the start of this section in *Curlew River* is seen in Example 40. In it, we see again how Britten has carefully blurred the line and avoided traditional Western harmony. A flutter-tone flute appears as an instrumental marker for the madwoman just before the ferryman asks about the strange noise up the highway. The first, distant occurrence of the madwoman's motive is shown in Example 41.

Example 40. A *Curlew River* choral style. Reprinted, by permission, from Benjamin Britten, *Curlew River* (London: Faber & Faber, 1965).

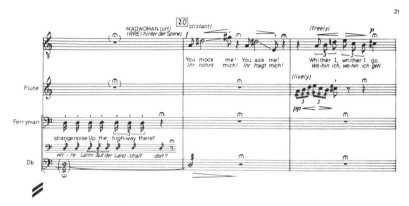

Example 41. The madwoman's motive in *Curlew River*. Reprinted, by permission, from Benjamin Britten, *Curlew River* (London: Faber & Faber, 1965).

THE HA NO MAEDAN

Issei

The waki and tsure of *Sumidagawa* move in silence to their correct sitting positions, and then the hayashi enters with an interlude lasting some three minutes and thirty seconds. At the third flute entrance, the shite appears on the ramp, wearing a dark hat that blocks one's view of the eyes of the mask. In addition to a white travelling robe over his costume, the shite has a bamboo branch in his right hand, an indication  of the woman's disoriented state. In *Curlew River*, the madwoman enters from backstage with disheveled hair and the white mask on the upper face as seen in Figure 26.

Sashi and *Issei*

In *Curlew River* the woman's first rambling thoughts are:

Where the nest of the curlew
Is not filled with snow,
Where the eyes of the lamb
Are untorn by the crow,
The carrion crow—
There let me, there let me, there let me go!

This text is not found in the noh play, but forms a unit that Britten is able to repeat near the end, thus fulfilling the Western need for balance. The music for this aria is a distorted folk-song-like melody set against the tremolo flute that is the madwoman's instrumental marker. The viola provides nontriadic harmony, with double stops of sevenths or fourths.

The first lines (sashi) of the madwoman in *Sumidagawa* are not quotes from a folk song, but come from a poem by Fujiwara no Kanesuke:[22]

> Although a mother's mind
> May be unclouded,
> She well may lose her way
> Through love of her child.

Before singing these lines, the madwoman, standing near the shite pillar, stamps her foot as a symbol of her high emotional state.[23] The flute is still heard at the start as a transition from the instrumental prelude into this vocal section. The power of the five-line sashi is conveyed with no further movements or gestures by the shite until the final line ("Does he not know his mother's grief?"), at which point the crying motion is made with the left hand. Musically, the lines are done in the soft (*yowa*) style in a relatively free rhythm (fuai) in relation to the drum accompaniment. The vocal range is narrowed to some three contiguous pitches, though two stereotyped melodic patterns on higher pitches occur at the end of the third and the beginning of the fourth lines of the text. Are these consonant with the Western concept of melody, in which a climax appears some two-thirds of the way through a period, after which the tension subsides? The words chosen for these patterns would not seem to support this, for one refers to white clouds and the other to the travellers to whom the madwoman is calling for help. Detailed explanations of the meaning of every phrase in the text can be found in the Japanese source books listed in note 12. To present these explanations in this study would interfere with our musical goals, but, to give the reader some sense of the constant wordplay that is characteristic of the tradition, let us explain this passage. The mention of white clouds involves a so-called hanging word (*kake kotoba*) in Japanese poetry, for the spoken word for cloud (*yuki*) could also refer to the travel (*yuki*) of the travelling (*michiyuki*) people (*bito*) of the next line. Perhaps the vocal high points of the music occur here for poetic reasons.

The issei section proper opens with a reference to yet another poem with double meanings:[24]

Does not the skyey wind
Whisper to the waiting pines?

The word for pine (*matsu*) also means a "pining heart," and so captures the spirit of the scene correctly as the shite sings the first line and the chorus replies with the second, while the madwoman stamps her foot again.

In this section of *Curlew River*, the woman moves about and eventually falls to the ground. She then engages in an exchange with the chorus, the last lines of which are:

Dew on the grass
Sparkles like hope.
It's here, it's gone!

Some of this text is repeated in the opening words of the transition into the dance that follows in the noh play.

Kakeri and *Sashi*

A *kakeri* is a form of dance used in noh for warlike or mad scenes. During the two-minute hayashi opening, the two major gestures of the shite are a pointing of the bamboo branch and a repeated foot stamp. In the sashi section, the woman sings "In this world fleeting like dews upon Makuzu Field,"[25] but does not move, though there is a foot stamp. The chorus completes her line lyrically with "Should I thus pass my days complaining of my bitter day?" while the shite turns slowly, looking for the lost child. As in other opening passages, the vocal line that follows is restrained and accompanied by some form of the standard mitsuji drum pattern. A different, *tsuzuke* drum pattern will not appear until the last of the remaining ten lines sung by the shite.[26]

Thus, the drum part, along with a flute entrance, will clearly mark the final cadence of a unit. I point this out simply to remind us that even in nonthematic, through-composed music the important musical truism holds that what makes a cadence a cadence is that something different happens.

The mother speaks of the kidnapping and her quest without movement. The high-pitched melodic pattern *haru* occurs in the sixth line on the word *seki* (barrier), which refers to areas she has passed, and in the ninth line on *omoi go no* (thinking of my son). Those who have read the earlier chapters of this book will know that the two renderings of such a pattern are not the same, though in this case they have a common tonal area and contour. Example 42 * is an attempt to notate the ninth line in a manner that will evoke its style, though listening to cassette example JJ is the best way of understanding the passage. The beat is elastic, not metronomic, so the tempo markings shown should not be taken literally, but should be considered as listening aids. In this example we see what is meant by a haru pattern in the voice and one of the ways a passage might be fitted into the eight-beat mitsuji drum pattern. As the drum pattern changes and the flute enters, the mother speaks of her desperate quest and weeps again.

Example 43 shows the restrained manner of the opening of this section in *Curlew River*. The section begins with a canonic trio for the flute, double bass, and singer. Other instruments enter, when the vanishing of the child is mentioned, to create a Western sense of climax. The use of this combination of dynamics and texture is Western, but note the constant horizontal (i.e., linear) design. It is so "right" for noh drama and for Western medieval or contemporary

Example 42. A kakeri passage from *Sumidagawa* (cassette example JJ).

music. Example 44 shows the *Curlew River* version of the text of Example 42. It is more restrained because earlier Britten has been quite dramatic. It also reflects the Western fascination with repeated or developed motives (cf. Example 43). In sum, though both versions

Example 43. A motive in a madwoman's aria in *Curlew River*. Reprinted, by permission, from Benjamin Britten, *Curlew River* (London: Faber & Faber, 1965).

Example 44. Development of the madwoman's-aria motive. Reprinted, by permission, from Benjamin Britten, *Curlew River* (London: Faber & Faber, 1965).

are effective, they illustrate two different aesthetics: the noh requires infrequent use of sonic or movement conventions that are common to the entire repertory, and Western drama concentrates on frequent use and development of motives that are peculiar to the specific composition.

Sageuta and Ageuta

In *Sumidagawa*, the text of the choral sageuta alludes to a work by the ninth-century Chinese poet Po Chu-i: "Though he be a thousand miles away—'tis said—that a mother never forgets her child." During this drum-accompanied song, the shite moves forward slowly, raises the bamboo stick, and then steps back. A drum interlude without movement or text gives one time for reflection until the first line of the choral ageuta, which continues the previous thought: "And yet the bond of parenthood cannot survive the grave." Apparently this was a Buddhist concept of the period. It most certainly is not a Christian one. At this point, the chorus suddenly slows down and sings the powerful line shown in Example 45*.[27] It then moves directly to the next line, about "four birds that left their nest."[28] At this moment the shite moves again. The flute enters, and the chorus sings a lyrical haru pattern to the line "Will my weary quest end here?" while the shite moves to face the waki and tsure, for the chorus next says that the woman has reached the Sumida River.

Example 46 shows the opening theme that Britten develops out of the material in Example 44 for the text of the sageuta. Since the ageuta text is too Japanese and Buddhist for a Christian parable, it is reduced to

Will her search be at end
Here, at the Curlew River,
Now she has reach'd the Curlew River?

Note the musical consistency of the single-note repetitions in a five-beat pattern.

Now that all characters have been introduced in both plays, the plot can be carried forward.

Example 45. An ageuta chorus passage from *Sumidagawa* (cassette example KK).

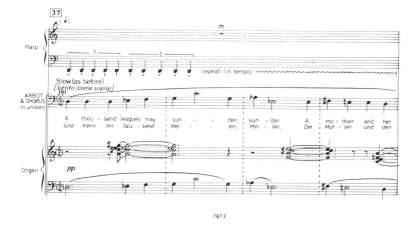

Example 46. A *Curlew River* choral passage. Reprinted, by permission, from Benjamin Britten, *Curlew River* (London: Faber & Faber, 1965).

THE HA NO CHŪDAN

Mondō

The function of this dialogue between the boatman and the woman is not easily transported into another culture. Dramatically it shows the boatman being converted from ridicule to sympathy. What is lost in translation is the poetic game that the author is playing with an informed audience. When the ferryman refuses to let the woman on his boat unless she dances, she replies:

> What a clumsy way of speaking! Since you are a Sumida ferryman, you should have answered, "Come on board, for the day is spent,"

> Yet you refuse a passage
> To me, a city lady.

What is particularly significant about her quotation is that it is from a famous ninth-century novel, the *Ise monogatari*, in which the author, Narihira, was also supposed to have crossed the Sumida River following this remark. The quotation thus allows the noh writer to combine pathos and literary skill. The woman quotes again from the same story:

> O birds of Miyako,
> If you are worthy of your name,
> Tell me does my love still live?

Originally about a lover, the inquiry is now about a child. The birds of far-off Kyoto (Miyako) are regional, but the madwoman argues that a white bird seen near the boat should not be called just a sea gull but rather a Miyako bird. This strange argument not only puts the boatman on his poetic mettle but also makes him aware of the depth of the woman's thoughts about her son.

Most of the dialogue of the mondō is done in stylized speech (kotoba), but when the boatman finally realizes the true situation, the drums return and the waki and shite enter into a most unusual and powerful call-response duet. The terms of love from the original poem are sung by the waki while the woman substitutes thoughts of her son:

Ferryman:	So Narihira long ago
Mother:	Asked, "Is she still alive?"
Ferryman:	Remembering his lady in Miyako.
Mother:	Moved by like yearning,
	I am seeking my lost child
	In the Eastland.
Ferryman:	To long for a sweetheart,
Mother:	To seek after a lost child,
Ferryman:	Both spring
Mother:	From love.

This increasingly dense exchange builds dramatically without great changes in the vocal lines until the last thought, "From love," which is sung lyrically.

In *Curlew River*, much more is made of the demand that the woman entertain before she can get on the boat. The chorus and characters build an intense polyphonic set of cries for entertainment, which ends, as seen in Example 47, in the first full choral sound of the piece. The conflict of class and dialect that dominated the Japanese text is rendered almost as a recitative in *Curlew River*. And what are Britten and Plomer to do with the grand Japanese tradition of dropping known quotations from ancient sources into the middle of action scenes? Plomer's solution is for the woman to say,

Let me remind you
Of the famous traveller
Who once made a riddle
In this very place.

Above a harp ostinato, a canon for singer and flute sets the text

"Birds of the Fenland, though you float or fly,
Wild birds, I cannot understand your cry.
Tell me, does the one I love
In this world still live?"

Example 47. The *Curlew River* choral passage "Show us what you can do!" Reprinted, by permission, from Benjamin Britten, *Curlew River* (London: Faber & Faber, 1965).

What the ferryman then calls gulls are called curlews by the woman, thus helping to set the event in England rather than Japan. The other characters and parts of the chorus then enter into imitational polyphony in which the double meaning of the poem is lost. The ferryman and traveller retain it in a call and response:

Traveller:	A traveller at this very place cried:
Mother:	"Tell me, does the one I love
	In this world still live?"
Traveller:	Thinking of his lady love—
Ferryman:	She too is seeking someone lost.
Traveller:	—Yearning for a woman.
Ferryman:	Searching for a son.
Traveller & Ferryman:	Both derive from longing,
	Both from love.

Before the last two lines are delivered, the chorus has entered as well.

Ageuta

This section of *Sumidagawa* is often seen separately in *shimai* dance recitals, so we should describe its action in more detail. Musically, the chorus enters in the strong style (tsuyo), repeating the first line:

O Miyako-bird, I too will ask you,
O Miyako-bird, I too will ask you,
Is my dear child still living
Somewhere in the Eastland?

Foot stamps by the shite mark the first statement of the word *Miya-kodori* (Miyako-bird), and a short hayashi interlude separates the repetitions of the line. The chorus then continues to sing the woman's thoughts:

I ask and ask, but it will not answer.
O rude Miyako-bird!

The dance involves glances to the left and right and then a movement forward in search of the child. The shite moves back towards the ramp as the chorus sings a quotation from the eighth-century poetry collection *Manyōshū*:

By the Horie River where boats hurry past each other,
Miyako-birds utter their cries.

The reference to those particular birds, to boats, and to cries is obviously appropriate to the moment in the play. Equally obvious is the meaning of the shite's pointing with his left hand in one direction and then another, for the chorus sings

> There at Naniwa in the West,
> Here by the Sumida in the East.

The shite moves onto the ramp and turns at the designated stopping spot, touching the brim of the hat at the words "How far I have come from home." The woman returns to face the ferryman, who has received a pole from one of the two "invisible" men (kōken) who sit at the back of the stage to assist with props and costumes. The woman pleads to be let on board with a gesture of the bamboo stick, and then kneels, clasps her hands, beats the stick on the floor, and drops it. During all this action, the chorus continues to sing forcefully. A ritard on the word *fune* (boat) is marked by two quick beats on the ō tsuzumi, one of the important standard signals in sung dance music that a final cadence is approaching. A similar two beats are heard in the "dance ending" (*kuse tome*) pattern of the ko tsuzumi that accompanies the next line, "Let me come on board." The entrance of the flute and the slowing of the tempo also tell us that the dance is ending.

The staging instructions for this section of *Curlew River* have the mother circling or reaching out for the birds while the chorus sings text similar to that of the noh and the flute plays the madwoman's motive. Her movements end in a supplication, to which the ferryman and traveller respond. The call "Let her aboard!" grows in density from the chorus and traveller while the woman holds her pleading position. The horn motive and drum signals of the ferryman are heard as he tells the woman and traveller to come aboard with all the "others." Throughout both stories, "other people" are part of the action, though the chorus in the noh never moves. In *Curlew River*, the boarding of the boat is an elaborate activity, complete with imitations of its tipping as people climb aboard. Part of Britten's intention is to "involve" the audience through stage action. The involvement in noh is achieved more through the mind.

Mondō

The waki accepts the new passenger in unaccompanied speech while the woman removes her hat. She and the traveller get on board in front of the waki in complete silence.

In *Curlew River*, after repetitions of the ferryman's motive and a prayer for safety that uses the chant cadence, the ferryman calls, "Hoist the sail!" and an instrumental interlude is heard as two acolytes raise a stylized sail. Then instrumental glissandi accompany a river-poling song sung by the ensemble. The text is filled with Western ideals:

> Curlew River, smoothly flowing
> Between the Lands of East and West,
> Dividing person from person!
> Ah, Ferryman, row your ferry boat!
> Bring nearer, nearer,
> Person to person,
> By chance or misfortune,
> Time, death or misfortune
> Divided asunder!

Katari

The traveller in both dramas asks the ferryman about the people on the other shore, and the ferryman tells the long story of how a year ago on this very day a slave trader brought a twelve-year-old boy here and left him to die. In *Sumidagawa* the monologue is rendered by the waki without accompaniment, motion, or obvious melody, though there are many stylistic nuances. Since the mother has removed her hat, one is  able to study the noh mask as the ferryman gives more information about the child. The ferryman's mention of the boy's name and his father's name and his final invocation of Amida Buddha affect a viewer's eyes or mind, for the expression on the mask seems to change though one sees no clear head or body motion. Finally the ferryman says:

> There may be some people from Miyako in this boat.
> Let them offer prayers for the repose of his poor soul,
> even if they are not relations of the dead lad.

At this point the shite makes the weeping gesture.

The text and mask are obviously the most powerful elements of this section of the noh drama. What happens in *Curlew River* at this point? The glissandi suggesting the boat's motion continue while the ferryman's horn and drum sounds accompany the beginning of the story. Throughout most of the recitativelike telling of this rather long tale, the organ plays restrained tone clusters. Periodically the ferryman poles the boat, for action is as essential in Western theater as nonaction is in noh drama. As the story progresses, the texture of the glissandi gradually thins from the sound of the double bass to that of the viola and then to that of the harp as the ferryman speaks of the boy's last "Kyrie eleison!" The chorus repeats this phrase using the chant motive from the opening of the parable. Another Christian addition to the story is the ferryman's statement that some people come to the boy's grave for healing and some have claimed to have seen the boy's spirit.

The journey ends, the sail comes down during an organ interlude, and the cross on the tomb is seen.[29] The river song is repeated by the chorus to give the scene a Western sense of completion. It is set against a plodding, descending instrumental line as all but the woman walk to the tomb.

Mondō

The traveller's statement of his decision to stay is still in unaccompanied-speech style, as is his dialogue with the boatman (which does not appear in the published noh utaibon). The traveller gets off the boat in silence as the ferryman moves closer to the weeping mother. When he asks her to leave, from behind the mask comes the muffled sounds of questions that gradually get louder and closer in timing to the ferryman's answers:

Mother:	What was the lad's age?
Ferryman:	Twelve.
Mother:	His name?
Ferryman:	Umewaka-maru.
Mother:	And his father's name?
Ferryman:	Lord Yoshida.
Mother:	Since then have neither of his parents been here?
Ferryman:	Nor any of his kin.
Mother:	Much less his mother!

Ferryman: No, that would have been out of the question.
Mother: No wonder, neither kin nor parent came.
                He was the child
                This mad woman is seeking.
                Is this a dream?
                O cruel fate!

In Example 48 * one sees the increasing density in the
mondō and the change to lyricism when the mother
asks about the boy's parents. However, the power of
the scene really comes from a combination of this
music with the stage setting and movement. In her
kneeling position the mother gradually turns towards
the boatman behind her. She drops her hat and weeps
during the last line. The ferryman's pole is quietly

taken from him by the stage assistant as he voices his recognition
that this is indeed the mother of the child. Standing behind her, he
slowly and silently pushes her to the tomb.

Example 48. A mondō passage from *Sumidagawa* (cassette example LL).

Example 49 shows a passage from this section in *Curlew River*. Note how the drum accompaniment is really imitative and thus quite unlike hayashi accompaniment except in texture. Tone clusters remain the characteristic vertical sonority. After the lines "He was the child / Sought by this madwoman," continuous organ arpeggios, with multipart interjections of the singers, back the mother's cry of "Am I dreaming?" This climax is very Western, and by Western standards very powerful. An aria of grief is now added to the original design. The woman's first thoughts, of birds, curlews, and lambs, give the work a Western sense of continuity. These are succeeded by mad thoughts that give the aria sudden movement, leading to a quiet rendition of the madwoman's motive that has permeated the piece (Example 41). Perhaps no scene in the entire story better shows how different but effective the noh and Western approaches to drama can be.

Example 49. A mondō passage from *Curlew River*. Reprinted, by permission, from Benjamin Britten, *Curlew River* (London: Faber & Faber, 1965).

THE HA NO ATODAN

Kudoki

A kudoki in Japanese music is usually
the most lyrical or sad section of a composition. In *Sumidagawa*, the text certainly is appropriate for such a setting:

> I had hoped against hope
> To find my child
> And now I have reached strange Azuma,[30]
> He is no more upon this earth;
> Naught but this mound remains.
> Oh, how cruel!
> Was it for this that he was born,
> To be taken from his native land,
> To the remotest part of Azuma,
> Only to become dust by the roadside?
> Does my dear child truly lie beneath this grass?

These moving lines are done without gestures by the shite, who
kneels facing the tomb. The first lines are sung slowly, mostly on one
pitch. The haru melodic pattern occurs on *satemo*, the first word of
the line translated as "Naught but this mound remains," and again
on the word *haru* of *haru no kusa* (spring grasses) in the last line.
Accompaniment is provided only by the flute, which enters in a
most unusual, evocative manner as seen in Example 50*. The example also shows how this passage leads to the next entrance of the
chorus.

In *Curlew River*, all ask the woman to let the ferryman lead her to the grave, with pleas that his soul may
be received in heaven. Example 51 shows the opening
of Britten's kudoki. The wavering line does remind one
of the wide, slow vibrato of noh music. The flute provides at once an instrumental marker for the madwoman and the sound of the noh, though I doubt that
this was conscious on Britten's part. The undulation
continues throughout the aria and is made suddenly
loud by other instruments as the mother cries out,

Did I give birth to him
To have him stolen
And carried far, far away,
Here to the Eastern Fens
To end as dust, dust,
To end as dust by the road?

Example 50. The shite and chorus entrances in the kudoki of *Sumidagawa* (cassette example MM).

Sageuta and *Ageuta*

In the second part of Example 50* the drums return and the chorus enters the sageuta with the mother's call

O you people there,
Dig up the sod

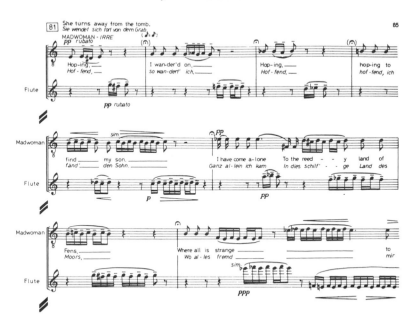

Example 51. The *Curlew River* kudoki aria. Reprinted, by permission, from Benjamin Britten, *Curlew River* (London: Faber & Faber, 1965).

So that I may once again
Gaze on his mortal form.

It is at this moment that the mother makes a sudden gesture upward with both her arms and then down in a digging motion, only to return her hands slowly to the mask in a weeping gesture. As the most active movements in the play so far, these gestures are particularly striking. They are an example of maximum effect from minimum material at its theatrical best, for no further movement occurs after the mother's hands drop from her face and a short hayashi interlude leads us to the ageuta.

Example 52. An excerpt from a chorus ageuta in *Sumidagawa* (cassette example NN).

Example 52* is a transcription from the ageuta of the passage on the course of human life to which the flute entrance adds such pathos. As the last line is repeated the mother returns to weeping. The chorus chants the Buddhist message of the tragedy:

He whose life was full of promise is gone,
And she whose life is worthless left behind.
Before the mother's eyes the son appears
And fades away
As does the phantom broom-tree.[31]
In this grief-laden world
Such is the course of human life.
The winds of death
Scatter the spring-time flowers of life;
The clouds of mutability
O'ercast the shining moon
That should light up the endless night of life and death.[32]
Now my eyes see how fleeting is this life.

The Buddhist message of the original text takes
nearly five minutes to perform in *Sumidagawa*, but it
is reduced to one minute in *Curlew River*, with the text

He whose life was full of promise
Promis'd, and is gone.
She who feels her life is passing,
She is left alone, and weeping.

These comments are made by the abbot and the chorus as seen in
Example 53. Time must be saved, for the Christian message is yet to
come.

Example 53. The choral equivalent of Example 52 in *Curlew River*. Reprinted, by
permission, from Benjamin Britten, *Curlew River* (London: Faber & Faber, 1965).

THE KYŪ NO DAN

Mondō

The ferryman admonishes the mother to chant rather than weep, but she cannot bring herself out of her grief. He holds a Buddhist chanting gong (a kane, called a *shōgo* in the text). In the videotape, he moves the hammer to strike it without actually doing so and then takes it to her, saying,

> However many people may gather together,
> It is a mother's prayers that will rejoice her dead child.

A drum-accompanied dialogue follows:

Mother:	I'll take the gong
	For the child's sake.
Ferryman:	Ceasing her moan, in a clear voice
Mother:	She prays with them under the shining moon.[33]
Ferryman:	Her thoughts wing straight
	To the Western Land of Bliss.

The shite and waki now enter into a rare duet, which is the well-known Buddhist prayer shown on the right.

> Adoration to countless million Buddhas,
> Each one Amida in the Western Paradise,
> The world of supreme bliss.

In *Curlew River*, the sound of a large bell marks the ferryman's plea that the mother seek prayers rather than tears. The traveller adds:

> Lady, remember,
> All of us here
> May pray for your child:
> But *your* prayer is best
> To rejoice his young soul.

As she agrees, a set of smaller, tuned Angelus type of bells ring and the chorus sings "The moon has risen." This phrase ends in a B-major chord—the first triad of the composition. Here is an example of maximum effect from minimum material at its Western best. The chorus continues:

> The river breeze is blowing,
> The Curlew River
> Is flowing to the sea.
> Now it is night
> And time to pray.

Each phrase is a step higher and ends on a triad, while the bells add their magic sound.

Nembutsu

While the chorus of *Sumidagawa* sings Buddha's name, the mother strikes the gong (though never on the beat of the chorus or the drums). The mother turns to the front and sings, in a highly lyrical style,

> From the Sumida
> Join in the voices
> Of the breeze and waves.

The chorus returns with Buddha's name (see illustration, p. 193) as the mother turns again to the tomb and strikes the gong. Then, again facing front, she says,

> True to their name,
> Miyako-birds join the choir.

The next choral chant of the sacred name is joined by the boy's voice and the flute as the mother returns to the tomb and strikes the gong.[34] The music stops and the mother says:

> Surely just now among them
> I heard my child's voice.
> He seems to be praying inside the mound.

The boatman replies:

> We, too, have heard your child.
> We shall keep silent;
> Say your prayer alone.

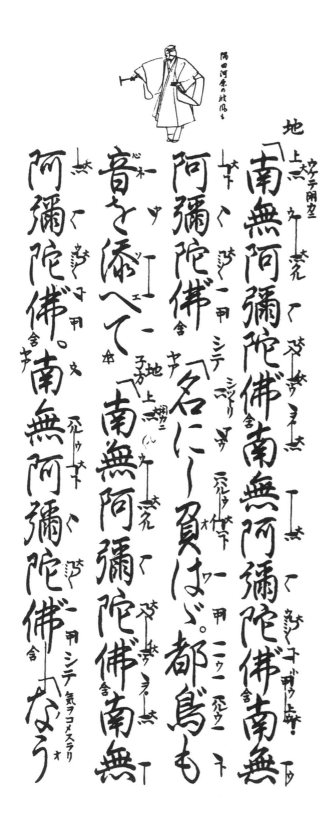

地
上 ウケテ開立

「南無阿彌陀佛南無阿彌陀佛南無
阿彌陀佛
音を添へて
「名に～頁はゞ。都鳥も
「南無阿彌陀佛南無
阿彌陀佛。南無阿彌陀佛
なう

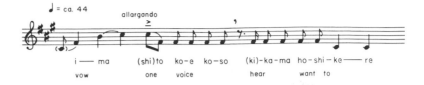

Example 54. The madwoman's call for the boy's voice in *Sumidagawa* (cassette example OO).

As seen in Example 54*, the mother sings unaccompanied the plea "Oh, that I might hear his voice but once again!" The gong is hit twice after this passage as a symbol of her frenzy to generate the blessed sound again.[35]

Uta (Kiri)

The boy repeats the prayer to drum accompaniment, and as the child actor (kokata) emerges from the tomb with black, flowing hair and dressed in white the chorus sings "See, his voice and shape!" The mother and son face each other.[36] The mother drops her gong and moves forward, but the child ducks first under her right arm and then under her left, and goes back to the tomb while the chorus sings (cassette example PP):

> And as she seeks to grasp it by the hand,
> The shape begins to fade away;
> The vision fades and reappears
> And stronger grows her yearning.
> Day breaks in the eastern sky.
> The ghost has vanished;
> What seemed her boy
> Is but a grassy mound

Lost on the wide, desolate moor.
Sadness and tender pity fill all hearts.
Sadness and tender pity fill all hearts.

The mother looks forward in despair and at the mention of yearning travels back towards her original spot, making a hugging gesture. She approaches the grave, reaches out, and drops before it with a weeping gesture as the last line is repeated. The tempo slows down, the flute enters as the desolate moor is mentioned, the pitch center drops to the lowest range, and a cadence is heard on the drums. Then there is silence.
The actors move slowly down the ramp, the chorus exits through its small side door, and then the hayashi leaves. No applause is heard; there is only a long period of silent meditation for those who have seen the play in its proper setting, one's own heart.

In *Curlew River*, the chorus enters with a Latin prayer, the first verse of which says,

> Praise in song those angels holy
> Whom our heavenly Father gave
> As our guides to watch and guard us
> From the cradle to the grave.[37]

While the chorus sings the hymn, the ferryman and traveller evoke all the saints, martyrs, and holy company, "There in the blessèd Abode of eternal Peacefulness." A flute marks the entrance of the mother, in bitonality against the chant as she is still in grief:

> From the river, I hear voices,
> Like souls abandoned
> Curlews are calling.

She then repeats text heard earlier in the parable:

> Wild birds, I cannot understand your cry.
> Tell me, does the one I love
> In this world still live?

As the chorus sings on through further verses of the hymn, a boy's voice, overlapping with the chorus, takes up its lines of Latin text. The mother notes the new voice, and the chorus and child continue their call and response. As the mother calls to hear the voice again, the child's voice overlaps with hers, and, after his "Amen," the chorus quietly gasps:

> Hear his voice!
> See, there is his shape!

A piccolo enters the ensemble to represent the boy, who appears and consoles his mother:

> Go your way in peace, mother.
> The dead shall rise again
> And in that blessèd day
> We shall meet in heav'n.

To this the chorus adds "Amen," set in a soft tone cluster. The instrumental ensemble enters with music like that of Example 37, while the monks hide the mother from view and the traveller and ferryman resume their monks' clothes. Then the abbot sings:

> Good souls, we have shown you here
> How in sad mischance
> A sign was given of God's grace.
> A vision was seen,
> A miracle and a mystery,
> At our Curlew River here.
> A woman was heal'd by prayer and grace,
> A woman with grief distraught.

The monks then join him in singing:

> O praise our God that lifteth up
> The fallen, the lost, the least;
> The hope He gives; and His grace that heals.

And the abbot concludes, "In hope, in peace, ends our mystery." The instruments are picked up and the entire group then processes off the stage along the ramp, singing the Latin hymn with which the parable began.

CONCLUSION

As a Western researcher, I, like the abbot of the parable, cannot leave endings open. With the images of this writing before me, let me first comment that, in trying to evoke our final view, much was revealed that before had been hidden from me. The sights and sounds of these two incredibly powerful theatrical events swirl through my mind like Miyako and curlew birds. The paths of their flights are parallel for only a short time. In the end, they seek different goals.

To give this study a Western sense of closure, let me add, finally, that seldom have I experienced two equally logical but different musical events that were so comparable. They are compliments to their composers and to the cultures that generated their structures and aesthetics. Perhaps writing about them has helped others see some of their hidden power and beauty. In any event, our mystery, too, is over.

POSTLUDE

Our views of Japanese music now must fade like the ghost of Umewaka-maru in *Sumidagawa*, but, as in the play, there is hope of some memory, some recall. In our circumambulation we began in the real but relatively unknown world of drum making. Even among its specific shapes and materials we found ambiguity in the criteria for a good drum and a beautiful sound. When we looked next at drum lessons, adumbrations of spiritual goals seemed to impart a more subtle color to our view of pedagogical methods.

When we sought insights into actual compositions under comparative scrutiny, our objects seemed to become even less tangible. Theatrical compositions like *Shakkyō* turn out to be better seen with an eye accustomed to the mountains of Japanese screen paintings, for their bases are solid but seldom visible. The path that led us through such musical mountain ranges often disappeared like some point in a Japanese painting. However, the inevitability of the movement on such paths became evident as we grew accustomed to moments of structural insecurity. The logic of Japanese musical forms was certainly evident by the time we had traversed the Stone Bridge of *Shakkyō* in both noh and kabuki styles and moved on to enjoy a picture of an urban festival as drawn in the nagauta concert piece *Kanda matsuri*. Once we had become aware of the manner in which performers' interpretations can change the shape of a piece like *Hōrai*, we were better able to view Japanese music as having a basic structure that allows for a sense of impermanence without the use of improvisation. Finally, we looked across centuries and cultural barriers to see how a powerful topic was handled with equal but different musical techniques in noh drama and in Benjamin Britten's parable.

In all, I rather think that Ernest Bloch might have enjoyed all these views, these cherished traditions that have not yet fossilized but rather have continued to be reshaped for new moments and new viewers. Only through such views can the evanescent nature of music be worthy of discussion in the memory of one of music's beloved Western practitioners. As we wander around the mount of music, giving special attention to lovely views selected from the plains of Japanese music, I hope that the shadows of our passing have brought pleasure to the spirit of Ernest Bloch. He began his journey along the trails and vistas of music some one hundred years ago. I thank him for leaving behind so many musical memories of his travels, and such useful guideposts towards particularly beautiful areas for further exploration.

NOTES

FIRST VIEW

1. For details see William Malm, *Japanese Music and Musical Instruments* (Tokyo: Tuttle, 1959), chapts. 4, 7, 9.

2. Hayashi Kenzō, "Butten ni awareta gakki, ongaku, buyō" [Indications of musical instruments, music, and dance in Buddhist literature], in *Tōdai no gakki* [Asian instruments], ed. Kishibe Shigeo, Koizumi Fumio, Hirano Kenji, and Yokomichi Mario, Tōyō ongaku senshō [Selected studies in Far Eastern music], vol. 2 (Tokyo: Ongaku no tomo sha, 1968), pp. 76–80.

3. Tanabe Hisao, *Nihon no gakki* [Japanese musical instruments] (Hyaku-shi: Hyaku shuppan, 1964), pp. 204–21. For Chinese characters, see Shimonaka Yasaburo, ed., *Ongaku jiten* [Music encyclopedia] (Tokyo: Heibonsha, 1965), vol. 6, p. 309.

4. Kikkawa Eishi, *Nihon ongaku no rekishi* [The history of Japanese music] (Osaka: Sōgensha, 1965), pp. 19–20.

5. Kishibe Shigeo, *Tōyō no gakki to sono rekishi* [Far Eastern musical instruments and their history] (Tokyo: Kōundō, 1948), pp. 213–15.

6. See further P. G. O'Neill, *Early Nō Drama* (London: Humphries, 1948), pp. 1–9.

7. For an opinion that the ō tsuzumi appeared first see Hagiwara Izumi, "Noh ni itaru taiko no hensen" [The change in drum types in noh], *Kanze* 10, nos. 8, 9 (1979): 23–30, 27–32.

8. Ikuta Shigeru and Yamazaki Gakudō, *Tsuzumi dō no kantei* [The evaluation of tsuzumi drum bodies] (Tokyo: Wanya, 1917).

9. This biography is based on an article in Shimonaka Kunihiko, ed., *Ongaku daijiten: Encyclopaedia Musica* (Tokyo: Heibonsha, 1982), vol. 5, p. 2618.

10. Manuscripts 2, 5, and 6 were first published in *Nōgaku* 10 (January 1912). All were edited by Kunisho Shinsaburō, who also wrote an introductory essay, "Tsuzumi no dō no kantei" [The evaluation of tsuzumi bodies].

11. The details of this preliminary description are verified by reference to Ikuta and Yamazaki's book or to the basic book on ko tsuzumi of the National Theater, Tanaka Denzaemon XI, *Narimono kyōsokuhon* [A percussion music reference book] (Tokyo: Kokuritsu gekijō, 1970), vol. 2.

12. The sensitivity of all ko tsuzumi heads to atmosphere can be noted during performance, for one often sees a ko tsuzumi drummer readjusting rope tension and breathing on the heads to restore humidity. Modern stages and their lighting and heating systems are particularly hard on ko tsuzumi heads. Experiments have been made in producing durable, thin plastic heads that produce strong *pon* tones under varying conditions. They work, but are weak in *ta* and *chi* sounds and so far have proved useful only in lessons and practice.

13. Ikuta and Yamazaki, *Tsuzumi dō no kantei*, sec. 1, p. 49.

14. Ikuta and Yamazaki, *Tsuzumi dō no kantei*, sec. 1, p. 51.

15. Zelkova and maple are also used.

16. Further fieldwork is necessary before any comments can be made on the conditions, locations, and ages of trees or the cuts of lumber that are believed to result in the best drums. However, from written materials on other Japanese instruments we know that such factors are important in the art of drum making.

17. The character for sea (*umi*) is sometimes used to indicate this bowl. To distinguish between internal and external shapes, I shall call the internal shapes the bowl and the tube and the external shapes the cylinder and the cup.

18. The character used to write the word *wan* for this curve is sometimes one meaning "to bend" rather than the character that denotes the bowl in general.

19. Ikuta and Yamazaki, *Tsuzumi dō no kantei*, sec. 1, p. 28.

20. For similar concerns in the making of other Japanese instruments see Malm, *Japanese Music*, pp. 177, 185.

21. The bowl surfaces of cheaper contemporary instruments are often unpolished. Sixteenth-century models often have deeper, less refined cuts but still can produce powerful tones.

22. See Ikuta and Yamazaki, *Tsuzumi dō no kantei*, sec. 1, pp. 92–131, sec. 3, pp. 155–73.

23. The horizontal lines are common in cheaper models today.

24. "Ko tsuzumi dōshimei oyobi kaname heidō no sunpō," pp. 155, 156. Photographs of the interiors and exteriors of drums by famous makers can be seen in Saito Yoshinotsuke, *Meibutsu ko tsuzumi taikan* [A general view of famous ko tsuzumi] (Tokyo: Nōgaku shorin, 1931).

25. By *to the left* or *to the right* is meant that the cut may not be a V, but may tilt so that one side of it is straight and the other side at an angle.

26. Concerning Michimoto, see "Dō meikan," p. 19.

27. Concerning Kiyosuke, see "Dō meikan," p. 39. The relationship of Kiyosuke to Yasuke is seen in Yamazaki's genealogical chart in Ikuta and Yamazaki's book.

28. Concerning the Katanami guild, see "Kyōjiki-shō," pp. 73–74.

29. Concerning the Orii guild, see "Kyōjiki-shō," pp. 58–60.

30. All the information in this paragraph is from Ikuta and Yamazaki's book.

31. Though we are concentrating on one area, drum shops extend much further in all directions. A study of the directory of Kooriyama, a suburb of Nara northwest of Sakurai, shows that place names still reflect the older traditions. There is a north and a south Carpenter Block (Daiku), a New Wood Block (Shinki), and even a Tsutsui Block, the first character of which is that for the body of a tsuzumi.

32. "Dō meikan," p. 3. The only comment on his style is that he preferred darker wood (*hakuboku sakura*). Much more information is available on the second generation of this line.

33. I am is particularly grateful to the head of the Miyamoto drum and festival material manufacturing firm, Miyamoto Yoshihiro. We studied the drum markings together and compared them with examples from his own, rare collection. The Kō guild of the Kanze school of noh tsuzumi players traces its beginnings to Miyamasu according to Kō Yoshimitsu in his *Ko tsuzumi no tomo ni* [Help in ko tsuzumi playing] (Tokyo: Wanya, 1968), p. 49.

SECOND VIEW

1. In my case, the reference work for the ko tsuzumi was Kō Yoshimitsu, ed., *Kō ryū ko tsuzumi seifu* [The correct notation of Kō guild ko tsuzumi music] (Tokyo: Nōgaku shorin, 1955), and for the taiko Komparu Sōichi, ed., *Komparu ryū taiko zensho* [A complete collection of Komparu guild taiko music] (Tokyo: Hinoki shoten, 1953). For the ō tsuzumi it was Tazaki Nobujiro, ed., *Kado no ryū ō tsuzumi kaitei* [A collection of Kado guild ō tsuzumi music] (Tokyo: Kinoki taikodō, 1925).

2. There is also a flute player, who uses the noh flute or a bamboo flute. However, except in passages heavily influenced by noh, the flute lines are seldom indicated in the drum part books, though sometimes there may be an indication of where the flute should enter.

3. It will also become evident as this series of essays progresses that one cannot necessarily predict what those other parts will be, since performers from different guilds will render the same passage in a different manner. See, in particular, the Fifth View.

4. A more germane analogy might be the tradition (ritual?) of a good noh actor, who must spend time looking at a mask before he puts it on so that he can become the character that it represents.

5. Colleagues have commented that almost all of Japanese personal relations have a ritualistic structure and language. However, I shall confine myself to experiences related to my topic.

6. Perhaps the best-known Western book on this topic is Eugen Herrigel, *Zen in the Art of Archery*, trans. R. F. C. Hull (New York: Pantheon, 1953).

7. Figures 9 and 10 are from Tanaka, *Narimono kyōsokuhon* vol. 2. Figures 11 and 12 are from volume 1 of that series.

8. Two early examples can be seen in William Malm, *Nagauta: The Heart of Kabuki Music* (Tokyo: Tuttle, 1963), pls. 2, 4.

9. *Shibui* can mean something astringent in drink, but in the arts refers to something quiet, sober, or refined in color.

10. I found that students could execute this position if they imagined that they were holding a helium balloon between their arms while playing drum patterns.

11. For details, see William Malm, "An Introduction to Taiko Music in the Japanese No Drama," *Ethnomusicology* 4, no. 2 (May 1960): 75–78. In Figure 13 (p. 45) Japanese notation for the taiko pattern kizami can be seen in the sixteen dots connected with lines at the top of the last column to the left. The drum calls appear above the appropriate dot to the left. An "extra" call above the first dot to the left shows that the notation is for the Kanze rather than the Komparu school of taiko playing.

12. See Fritz van Briessen, *The Way of the Brush* (Tokyo: Tuttle, 1962), pp. 31–39, 44–48.

13. It is quite common in Japan for one to learn an entire piece without ever hearing what the other drummers are doing. Sometimes the experience of playing within an ensemble occurs for the first time in one rehearsal or perhaps only at the moment of one's debut! Ō tsuzumi students usually learn their music by clapping their hands and may actually hit the drum for the first time only at such a recital; I was told by one student that it was quite a shock when all that sound came out. Think how much more complex the first experience of playing with other drummers must be.

14. These are *Yatai, Shoden, Kamakura, Shichōme*, and again *Yatai*.

15. See the "secret" notation of B3 in Hirano Kenji and Fukushima Kazuo, eds., *Sources of Early Japanese Music* (Tokyo: Benseisha, 1978), pp. 37–38. I have in my office a 1748 copy of fourteenth-century notation of flute parts for secret pieces from the komagaku and sarugaku traditions. Except for wormholes, it is quite clear.

16. Some insights into the deeper structure of music and music lessons may be acquired by studying the writings of Zeami Motokiyo as translated with commentaries by Izutsu Toshihiko and Izutsu Toyo in *The Theory of Beauty in the Classical Aesthetics of Japan* (The Hague: Nijhoff, 1981).

17. Malm, *Japanese Music*.

INTERLUDE

1. For an introductory essay, see Malm, *Japanese Music*, chap. 4, or Minagawa Tatsuo, "Japanese Noh Music," *Journal of the American Musicological Society* 10, no. 3 (Fall 1957): 181–200.

2. The standard beginner's books, both by Miyake Kōichi, are *Fushi no seikai* [The true understanding of melody] (Tokyo: Hinoki shoten, 1955) and *Jibyōshi no seikai* [The true understanding of basic rhythm] (Tokyo: Hinoki shoten, 1954).

3. The insights on this topic of Yokomichi Mario, Japan's leading scholar of noh music, are found in English in Frank Hoff and Willi Flindt, *The Life Structure of Noh* (Tokyo: Nōgaku shorin, n.d.), which originally appeared in 1974 issues, volumes 3 and 4, of *Concerned Theatre Japan*.

4. For drawings, see Malm, *Japanese Music*, p. 227.

5. See further Malm, *Nagauta*, chap. 3.

6. Tanabe, *Nihon no gakki*, pp. 145–48.

7. The historical displacement of these terms is shown in William Malm, "The Musical Characteristics and Practice of the Japanese Noh Drama in an East Asian Context," in *Chinese and Japanese Music-Drama*, ed. J. Crump and W. Malm, Michigan Papers in Chinese Studies, no. 19 (Ann Arbor: Center for Chinese Studies, University of Michigan, 1975), p. 101.

8. Convenient graphic examples of such melodic styles are seen in Miyake, *Fushi no seikai*.

9. Read the Conclusions in Malm, *Nagauta*, pp. 213-19.

10. A discussion in English of this less conventional Japanese use of the term *tetrachord* is found in Koizumi Fumio, "Musical Scales in Japanese Music," in *Asian Music in an Asian Perspective*, ed. Koizumi Fumio, Tokumaru Yoshihiko, and Yamaguchi Osamu (Tokyo: The Japan Foundation, 1977), pp. 73-79. Modern indigenous music theories are increasing. For example, Koizumi wrote the theory section of *Nihon no ongaku* [Japan's music] (Kishibe Shigeo, Kikkawa Eishi, Koizumi Fumio, Hoshi Akira, and Yokomichi Mario, contributors [Tokyo: Kokuritsu gekijō, 1974]), a brochure put out by the National Theater for educational purposes. This section has also appeared in Koizumi's *Nihon no ne* [Japanese sounds] (Tokyo: Seijisha, 1977), pp. 235-302.

11. See Miyake, *Jibyōshi no seikai*.

12. One of the first such works was the preface by Uji Kaganojō (1635-1711) to *Takenokoshū* [A Collection of bamboo shoots] of 1683. Takemoto Gidayū (1651-1714) himself provided theoretical materials at the start of *Jōkyō yonen gidayū danmonoshū* [Gidayū selections of Jōkyō fourth year] of 1687. These are available in Nishiyama Matsunosuke, ed., *Kinsei geidō ron* [Essays in premodern arts] (Tokyo: Iwanami shoten, 1972), vol. 61.

13. A good beginning source is Tanabe Hisao, *Hōgaku no tame no ongaku riron* [Music theory for traditional Japanese music] (Tokyo: Hōgakusha, 1977). Another source is Koizumi's article in Kishibe et al., *Nihon no ongaku*.

14. For a convenient survey of this "foreign" music in Japan, see Robert Garfias, *Music of a Thousand Autumns* (Berkeley and Los Angeles: University of California Press, 1975). Though this tradition became quite "Japanized," the fundamental continental approach to such things as meter and form seems to remain.

15. See Kineya Tokichirō, *Nagauta no sōhō* [Nagauta accompaniment] (Tokyo: Kōundō, 1932), pp. 111-13.

16. Tokumaru Yoshihiko has made frequent use of the term *heterophony* in relation to shamisen vocal music. For his discussion of the instrument, see "Some Remarks on the Shamisen and Its Music," in *Asian Music in an Asian Perspective*, pp. 90-99.

17. See Seihoui Matsuoka, ed., *Ma* (New York: Cooper-Hewitt Museum, 1979).

18. In Hirano and Fukushima, *Sources of Early Japanese Music*, compare the examples on pages 87-110 with those on pages 134-51.

19. See Monica Bethe and Karen Brazell, *Nō as Performance*, East Asia Program Papers, no. 16 (Ithaca, N.Y.: China-Japan Program, Cornell University, 1978), app. H, pp. 161-62.

20. A discussion and Japanese notation of these four patterns are found on pages 8 and 9 of the booklet included in the recording *Hōshō ryū mai no hayashi* [Drum music for dances of the Hōshō school], ed. Komparu Sōeman, Masuda Shōzō, and Hōshō Fusao (Victor SJL 180-183).

21. Books of such notation for the various schools of instrumentalists are available through the publishers Hinoki shoten and Wanya in Tokyo. Individual pieces or entire sets can usually be purchased. The mnemonics of the flute are written within the drum music in Figure 13, in the fifth and ninth columns from the right.

22. The excerpt is from the piece *Jo no mai* in Morita Misao, ed., *Yōkyoku mai hyōshi taisei* [A compilation of rhythm for noh dance music] (Osaka: Yoshida tokyoku shoten, 1914). Other examples of this notation are found in Malm, *Japanese Music*, p. 266, and in Stanley Sadie, ed., *New Grove Dictionary of Music and Musicians* (London: Macmillan, 1981), vol. 9, p. 537.

23. See Hirano and Fukushima, *Sources of Early Japanese Music*, pp. 163-67.

24. All the dances are reduced to a few pages in Komparu, *Komparu ryū*, pp. 254-58. The earliest surviving example of noh hayashi notation is the *Komasayoshi denshō* [The traditions of Komasayoshi] of around 1570. On pages 150-51 of Hirano and Fukushima, *Sources of*

Early Japanese Music, is a songbook of 1658 in which names of drum patterns and dots representing strokes can be seen.

25. See further Richard Emmert, "Hiranori," in *Musical Voices of Asia*, ed. Richard Emmert and Minegashi Yuki (Tokyo: The Japan Foundation, 1980), pp. 100–107.

26. This can be heard in the album *Noh*, ed. Yokomichi Mario (Victor SJ 3006), vol. 2, in an unusual pedagogical section on record 3, side 2, *Yōkyoku no samazama* [Various things about noh singing].

27. Examples of this style in grid-column notation and shorthand are found in Tanaka, *Narimono kyōsokuhon*, vol. 2, p. 59.

28. See James Brandon, *Five Kabuki Plays* (Cambridge: Harvard University Press, 1975), p. 359. See also Tanaka Denzaemon XI, *Hayashi* (Tokyo: Tamagawa University Press, 1983), pp. 200–233.

29. Seven shamisen notations from 1664–1842 are studied (with English summaries) and examples recorded in the album *Shamisen kofu no kenkyū* [A study of old shamisen notation], supervised by Hirano Kenji (Toshiba EMI THX-9021-17).

30. See Malm, *Japanese Music*, pp. 273–74.

31. Whenever I notate Japanese vocal lines in shamisen music, I am somewhat amused to note that they end up looking like a jazz singer's part with all their notated (not sung) syncopations.

32. Of course there are modern scores in Western notation, particularly of music in the gagaku tradition.

33. *He* is the correct word, for no female composers are known in the traditions studied, though some have existed in recent decades. Undoubtedly, there are many in the world of geisha music, but unfortunately that is not our topic, nor have I been able to do any research in that area.

THIRD VIEW

1. Fujimura Tsukuru, ed., *Nihon bungaku daijiten* [The encyclopedic dictionary of Japanese literature] (Tokyo: Shinchōsha, 1950–52), vol. 3, pp. 457–58.

2. The son of Ōe Saikō, he was known for his literary accomplishments. He became the Buddhist priest Jakujō in 988 and went to China in 1002. He died in the Sung capital of Lin'an in 1034.

3. In the commentaries on the shamisen version of this piece such as *Nagauta zenshū* [A complete nagauta collection] (Tokyo: Shuchan fushitsuke, 1939), the mountain is identified as the T'ien T'ai Shan of Chekiang, but a more probable choice would seem to be the Wu T'ai Shan in Shansi, since this is the traditional home of the Manjusri Bodhisattva in Chinese Buddhism, and Manjusri is the central Buddhist character in the plot.

4. This attribution is found in the 1765 *Nihyakujū-ban utai mokuroku* [An index of 210 noh vocal pieces], which is reprinted in National University Language and Literature Association, eds., *Kokugo kokubungaku kenkyūshi taisei zohō* [An enlarged compendium of historical studies of national language and literature] (Tokyo: Sanseido, 1977), vol. 9, p. 161. *Shakkyō* is listed as anonymous in Minoru Nishio, Yokomichi Mario, and Omote Akira, eds., *Nihon koten bungaku taikei* [A series of Japanese classical literature] (Tokyo: Iwanami shoten, 1963), vol. 41, p. 358.

5. O'Neill, *Early Nō Drama*, p. 28.

6. See the special magazine issue on folk lion dances *Geinō geijitsu* [The art of theatricals] 3, no. 1 (1930), and also Theatrical Research Department, eds., *Shishi no buyō* [Lion dances], no. 117 (June 1975), of the National Theater, Tokyo. In Japanese encyclopedias, discussions of general lion dances are usually found under the term *shishi-mono* (lion things), whereas lion dances from the noh and kabuki tend to be discussed under the term *shakkyō-mono*.

7. For the texts of surviving pieces, see Mori Jiichiro, ed., *Nihon buyō kyoku shūran* [A collection of pieces accompanying Japanese classical dance] (Tokyo: Shoshisha, 1965), under the titles listed. Note that the shamisen genre of *Kuruwajishi* is *kiyomoto* and that of *Azumajishi* is *tokiwazu*. The 1738 *Shakkyō*, sometimes called *Tsukaijishi*, survives as a *jiuta* koto-shamisen

piece only. Some pieces, such as *Kakubeijishi*, use more than one genre, a performance style called *kakeai*. However, most of the present lion pieces are in the nagauta repertory.

8. A discussion of the variety of theater lion dances is found in Kikkawa Eishi, ed., *Kikan hōgaku* [The traditional music quarterly], nos. 28, 29 (September, December 1982).

9. In kabuki these chases are more playful than ferocious, more of a household kitten than of an Asian lion.

10. See Malm, *Nagauta*, p. 18.

11. The composer later rose in rank within the guild system of nagauta to the title of Kineya Rokuzaemon X. We shall use the name that he carried at the time of this composition, though he is better known by his later name.

12. Kineya Eizō, *Nagauta no utaikata* [The singing of nagauta], 2 vols. (Osaka: Sōgensha, 1932), p. 453.

13. For more about the so-called *ōzatsuma-te*, see Malm, *Nagauta*, or the record notes of *Ōzatsumabushi* (Victor SJ 3018-3019).

14. Asakawa Gyokuto, "*Shakkyō* no kenkyū" [A study of *Shakkyō*], *Nihon ongaku* [Japanese music] 49 (1952): 16.

15. The closest version located was that of the now defunct Noda subguild of the Kanze school. The nagauta text used is found in any collection of nagauta notation or texts. Its romanization is based on the printing in Yoshizumi Kosaburō, ed., *Nagauta shin-keikobon* [A new practice book for nagauta] (Tokyo: Hōgakusha, 1955), vol. 5, no. 5. The translation and notes that follow were done by John R. Mayer in 1980, when he was a graduate student in Far Eastern languages at the University of California, Berkeley. Additional help was given later by Dr. Thomas Hare of Stanford University when he was a graduate student in Far Eastern languages and literature at the University of Michigan.

16. This is a special name (Clear, Cool Mountain) for the Five-Peak Mountain (Wu T'ai Shan) mentioned in note 3 above. It has some three hundred temples and was a favorite pilgrimage site for Pure Land (Jōdo) Buddhists during the Sung dynasty (960−1279), when Ōe lived.

17. The text is naturally filled with the conventions of noh literary style such as pivot words (*kake kotoba*) with two meanings and quotations from or allusions to lines from Chinese or Japanese poems. For example, line 11 is from a Chinese poem, and the veiled footprints of line 15 (*kumo mata ato*) are from a Japanese poem. The word *shiranami* in line 16 is a pivot word, for one expects *shirazu* (I do not know), but the possessive-case sign *no* connects white waves (*shiranami*) to the valley (*tani*). Another example of such word games is seen in lines 70−71, where *mo shirazu* would have meant "perhaps," but we end up with the sound of white waves. These examples are given in order to catch the tone of the play as it might be heard by a connoisseur.

18. This is a reference to a poem by Ōe Chōkō, based on a Chinese tale about a man out to cut wood who stopped to watch two boys play a game of go. Though he thought that he had stayed only half a day, the handle of his ax had rotted away in the years that he had remained there.

19. Manjusri (*Monju*) is the Bodhisattva for wisdom, literature, music, language, and youth and is thus worthy of respect from a literary priest on his way to collect sacred scriptures.

20. This proverb may be from the Brahmajāla-sutra: "It is as if an insect inside the body of a lion eats the lion's meat for himself without any other insects present." The Manjusri Bodhisattva is often pictured on the back of a lion. In the sutra, the lion represents Buddhist teaching as a whole. An individual believer, though small as an insect by comparison, may do great harm to the religion if careless with its precepts. Here, the passage is comparing the great adepts of the past to the lion and, likening the Stone Bridge to the small insect, says that even a task that seems so trivial can end in disaster if one is not suitably prepared to accomplish it.

21. In Shinto mythology, the divine couple Izanagi and Izanami are said to have come to earth on a bridge of rain and dew called the floating bridge of heaven (*ama no ukihashi*).

22. *Bugaku* is a generic term for court dancing. This passage could be interpreted to mean that the lion (*shishi*) dances *Toraden*, a famous large piece (*taikyoku*) imported in the T'ang

dynasty into the Chinese repertory (*tōgaku*) of the Japanese court. See Tanabe Hisao, *Nihon ongaku kowa* [A discussion of Japanese music] (Tokyo: Iwanami shoten, 1926), p. 553.

23. "The Lion Throne" refers to the throne of Manjusri.

24. The noh-flute player used in the recording is Teria of the Morita guild. The nagauta flutist, though not named on the recording, is probably Fukuhara of the Mochizuki school of hayashi.

25. These recordings are, respectively, *Noh: Shakkyō* (King KHA 19), *Shakkyō* (Chikuma VP 3022), in *Hōgaku taikei* [An outline of Japanese music], vol. 9, and *Shakkyō* (Columbia CLS 5099).

26. In addition to the source given in note 15 above, it is available in Bunka-fu notation 3350 (Tokyo: Hōgakusha, 1952 and 1981). Note that the performance version of the piece is not precisely the same as the notated version.

27. Its use in the lion dance will be discussed later.

28. For other examples of the use of B-flat in nagauta, see William Malm, "The Four Seasons of the Old Mountain Women," *Journal of the American Musicological Society* 31, no. 1 (Winter 1978): 81–117.

29. See Malm, *Japanese Music*, p. 229.

30. Tanabe Hisao, *Hōgaku yōgo jiten* [A dictionary of traditional Japanese music terms] (Tokyo: Tokyodō, 1975), p. 189.

31. Nogami Toyoichirō, ed., *Yōkyoku zenshū* [A complete collection of noh vocal music] (Tokyo: Iwanami shoten, 1935), p. 360. There are several kinds of raijo, and the one referred to in this case can be found in pieces other than *Shakkyō*.

32. Nagauta concert ensembles can vary from full groups to just one singer and one shamisen.

33. Tanabe Hisao uses these two terms in describing ranjo in his *Hōgaku yōgo jiten* (p. 195). Ejima Yūichi, in the booklet (p. 7) accompanying the recording *Hōshō ryū mai no hayashi*, discusses three parts, for he subdivides Tanabe's first section into mountain-echo music (kodama) and the open "dew" sound. One can say "open" not only because of the sound but also because another reading of the character for dew is "open" (*awara*). His third section is then the entrance of the lion (tōjō).

34. In learning to perform this passage, the space between the events is best measured by deep breathing.

35. See Malm, *Japanese Music*, p. 229. Also note the divisions listed in note 33 above.

36. Komparu, *Komparu ryū*, p. 267.

37. Komparu, *Komparu ryū*, p. 268.

38. Yokomichi is Japan's leading scholar on noh music. I thank Dr. Thomas Hare of Stanford University for showing me his notes on Yokomichi's lectures in Japan and also for his own insights into noh.

39. A powerful example can be seen by looking at the diagrams of the kakari and first three dan of the twelve noh dances in Komparu, *Komparu ryū*, pp. 254–57. The same cadencing patterns sweep across them all.

40. For a discussion of the placement of beat 1 in these examples, see Malm, *Nagauta*, pp. 88–89. For traditional notation of Example 13a, see Figure 13, the fifth column from the right.

41. The Kanze name for a drum guild is not quite the same as a Kanze school name, so a Kanze drummer can play in other schools as is done in this recording. The textbook for that school is Kanze Genshin, *Kanze ryū taiko tetsuke* [Taiko rhythm patterns for the Kanze school] (Tokyo: Wanya, 1959).

42. *Kanze ryū mai no hayashi* [Dance music for the Kanze school], ed. Komparu Sōemon and Masuda Shōzō (Victor SJL 111–115), record 5, side 1, band 2.

43. The term *dan* is sometimes used generically to mean a section, without regard to its formal meaning. Thus the first dan listed in the shamisen notation could be considered as a combination of the kakari and the first dan. However, in Mochizuki Tainosuke, *Kabuki geza ongaku* (Tokyo: Engeki shuppansha, 1975), p. 28, the drum music for this section is listed in

terms of five dan only, and their lengths are the same as those that the author arrived at independently.

44. In the shamisen notation, there is a melodic line written for use if the hayashi is not present at a performance. The tome patterns used by the taiko are *uchi kome*, *uchi kaeshi*, and kashira. This combination is standard for the final endings as distinct from the earlier dan endings.

45. The chief (*iemoto*) of the Semba guild, Semba Kōyū, kindly showed the author a handwritten copy of this notation.

46. Dan 3 is marked as beginning at this point in the shamisen notation.

47. *Shamisen no uta no oitachi to sono utsurikawari* (Columbia AL 5019-5022), side 5. For another early jiuta *Shakkyō* hear side 5 of *Shamisen ongaku koto hajime* [The beginnings of shamisen music] (CBS/Sony SOJZ 31-36).

48. *Nihon buyō ongaku* [Japanese dance music] (Victor SJ 3013, 1-3), vol. 1, record 2, side B, band 1. Hear also *Kamigata no gei, Edo no gei* [The art of Kyoto/Osaka and the art of Tokyo] (Columbia CLS 5053).

49. From the notation as found in Yoshizumi, *Nagauta shin-keikobon*, vol. 4, no. 1.

50. Listen to the recording *Shin-shakkyō* (Victor SLR 557).

51. For a discussion of such standard taiko sequences, see William Malm, "An Introduction to *Taiko* Music in the Japanese *Nō* Drama," Ethnomusicology 4, no. 3 (September 1960): 75-78.

FOURTH VIEW

1. Atsumi Seitarō, ed., *Hōgaku buyō jiten* [A dictionary of Japanese classical dance music] (Tokyo: Fuzambō, 1956), p. 137.

2. Kikkawa, *Nihon ongaku*, p. 307. The piece was actually the second of two compositions produced under the title *Momoyogusa*, "Grasses of a Hundred Nights." The first piece, by Hani Momosui, described the origin of chrysanthemums. It is not in the surviving repertory.

3. Kikkawa, *Nihon ongaku*, p. 307.

4. Dancers looking for new music often usurp nagauta concert pieces. This was done to *Kanda matsuri*.

5. Concerning these festivals, see Ono Takeo, *Edo no saiji fuzokushi* [Popular seasonal customs of Edo] (Tokyo: Tenbōsha, 1973), pp. 243-44, 320-28.

6. For some musical aspects of the Gion festival, see William Malm, "Music Cultures of Momoyama Japan," in *Warlords, Artists, and Commoners*, ed. G. Elison and B. Smith (Honolulu: University Press of Hawaii, 1981), pp. 161-85.

7. The text is derived from the music as published in Yoshizumi, *Nagauta shin-keikobon*, vol. 8. The translation was done by George Gish, Jr., in 1967, when he was a graduate student in Japanese studies at the University of Michigan.

8. For example, the first seven lines are all seven plus five in the Japanese manner of syllable counting.

9. Tanabe Hisao, *Shamisen ongakushi* [The history of shamisen music] (Tokyo: Soshisha, 1963), p. 118.

10. See the Third View. For a table of shamisen genres, see *Encyclopedia Britannica*, 15th ed., s.v. "Music, East Asia."

11. The magic kettle in line 9, was apparently a toy or souvenir sold on the street. It is found in folktales about an old priest turned badger named Shikaku who had a magic teakettle that never emptied, no matter how much water was poured from it. See *Nihon kokugo daijiten* [An encyclopedia of Japanese national language] (Tokyo: Shōgakkan, 1975), vol. 17, p. 577.

12. See Malm, "Four Seasons," pp. 88-89.

13. Recall from the Interlude that the pitch at which the music is set is arbitrary. Recall also that the vocal line is very much open to interpretation. It has not been included in the transcriptions of this section because it is not necessary to the understanding of our analytical points.

14. See William Malm, "The Modern Music of the Meiji Era," in *Modernization and Japan in the Humanities*, ed. D. Shively (Princeton, N.J.: Princeton University Press, 1971), chap. 7.

15. The story is better known in the West as a Chinese tale. According to Professor James Crump of the Department of Far Eastern Languages and Literature at the University of Michigan, the earliest mention of the drum is found in the biography of Wang Tsun in the Nan-shu of the Han dynasty (207 B.C.–A.D. 220). There are claims of its earlier use by the legendary emperors Yai and Shun. The moss on the drum may have been an addition of poets in the T'ang dynasty (618–907), at which time the legend may have been passed on to Japan.

16. The source is a tape taken by the author of a recital in Tokyo that is thought to be that given by the nagauta Seimei-kai on September 21, 1956, in Mitsukoshi Hall. The drummers were in the Tanaka guild. Only the shamisen line can be found in printed notation.

17. See Malm, *Nagauta*, pp. 100–101, 314–23.

18. See the flute transcriptions in William Malm, "*Shoden*: A Study of Tokyo Festival Music," *Yearbook of the International Folk Music Council* 7 (1976): 44–66.

19. For gong patterns, see Malm, "*Shoden*."

20. These lines are derived from lessons given the author by Wakayama Taneo, head of the Edo (not the Kanda) guild of matsuri bayashi. For complete transcriptions of the piece, see Malm, "*Shoden*."

21. Keep in mind that the transcription is an Edo matsuri beginner's version and the recording is of Kanda matsuri professionals.

22. See, for example, measures 90–93 of *Tsuru kame* in Malm, *Nagauta*, p. 252.

23. Listen to *Edo no kagura to matsuri bayashi* [Tokyo Shinto theatricals and festival music] (Victor SJ 3004), side 3, band 1, and see page 43 of the record notes, by Honda Yasuji.

24. For example, *Echigojishi* (1811). This is the piece Puccini borrowed from in *Madame Butterfly*.

25. *Kanda matsuri*, (Toshiba JHO 1010), side 1.

26. Yoshizumi, *Nagauta shin-keihobon*, vol. 8, p. 7, line 2.

27. See Kawatake Shigetoshi, ed., *Engeki hyakka daijiten* [An encyclopedia of the theatrical arts] (Tokyo: Heibonsha, 1960), vol. 3, p. 399. The dance is believed to have originated at the Sumiyoshi shrine in Osaka and then been spread around the country by itinerant *kanjin* ("alms solicitors"). The best-known offspring of the Sumiyoshi tradition is the dance *Kappore*.

28. The mnemonics of wataribyōshi are found in Malm, *Nagauta*, p. 87, and the pattern is seen in Brandon, *Studies in Kabuki* (Honolulu: University Press of Hawaii, 1978), p. 152.

29. For detailed analysis of a kudoki section, see Malm, *Nagauta*, pp. 187–92.

30. The so-called *chiri kara byōshi*. See p. 47.

31. Compare *Edo no kagura*, side 5, band 2, and also the recording *Edo kiyari* [Firemen's songs of Edo] (King KHA 1001).

32. Note that this does not indicate the return of any thematic materials. This is nagauta, not sonata, form.

33. For a study of dangire endings, see Malm, *Nagauta*, pp. 69–71. The one used in this piece is seen in Example 9c of that source.

FIFTH VIEW

1. Asakawa Gyokuto, *Nagauta hikikata utaikata* [The playing and singing of nagauta] (Tokyo: Daidōkan, 1936), p. 123. Since many of our commentaries are derived from this book, references to it will henceforth be made in the text rather than in footnotes if only a page reference is required. The contents of this book were included verbatim in Asakawa's *Nagauta meikyoku yōsetsu* [An explanation of famous nagauta pieces] (Tokyo: Hōgakusha, 1980). His remarks about *Hōrai* are found on pages 289–91 of the latter work. My text references are to the original edition.

2. For text examples from such sources, see Liza Crihfield, *Ko-uta: "Little Songs" of the Geisha World* (Tokyo: Tuttle, 1979).

3. The text and notation are from Yoshizumi, *Nagauta shin-keikobon*, vol. 2. The translation was done by David Hughes in 1975, when he was a graduate student at the University of Michigan, and was revised by him in 1982.

4. The oldest surviving Japanese song text that mentions Mount Hōrai is in the *imayō* genre and dates from the early fifteenth century. See Takano Tatsuyuki, *Nihon kayōshi* [The history of Japanese vocal music] (Tokyo: Shunjusha, 1926), p. 278. On page 107 of Atsumi's *Hōgaku buyō jiten*, Hōrai is shown to figure in other traditions such as *jiuta*, *utazawa*, and *kato bushi*, as well as in the name of a koto piece of the Yamada school.

5. The poem is number 390 in volume 4 of the *Shin kokin wakashū*, as found in Iwanami Yūjirō, ed., *Nihon koten bungaku taikei* (see the Third View, n. 4), vol. 28 (1977), p. 105.

6. The recording came out in at least two releases. One is as volume 12 of *Yoshimura dokugin shū* [A collection of solo performances by Yoshimura] (Columbia CLS 5175), and the other is the recording listed.

7. This is number 16 in a set entitled *Kineya Satoyo nagauta zenshū* [A complete collection of Kineya Satoyo nagauta performances] and is identified as a dance accompaniment.

8. On its tenth anniversary, the Tōon kai printed a survey of its goals and history, Matsushima Shōjurō, ed., *Tōon kai junen* (Tokyo: Tōon kai, 1967).

9. For further information on the Kensei kai and other modern movements, see Kikkawa Eishi, *Nihon ongaku*, p. 380, or Machida Kashō and Ueda Ryōnotsuke, eds., *Gendai hōgaku meikan, nagauta hen* [Famous modern Japanese music musicians, nagauta section] (Tokyo: Kabushiki kaisha hōgaku to buyō, 1966), pp. 139–57.

10. Because of the plethora of persons having the same professional family name, I must refer to some musicians by personal names.

11. Kineya Eizō, *Nagauta no utaikata* [The singing of nagauta], 2 vols. (Osaka: Sōgensha, 1932). The book resulted from four years of articles in the Sunday *Mainichi* newspaper. As with Asakawa (see n. 1 above), references to commentaries in this book will be made by page number.

12. The genealogical charts and short histories of all the schools and branches of the nagauta professional world will be found in Machida and Veda, *Gendai hōgaku*.

13. A striking symbol of this professional split is found in the fact that the first Jōkan used new characters to write the family name Kineya. The reader must realize by now that most of the persons mentioned in this survey are worthy of extensive separate biographies, but we must leave that fascinating legacy to some other book or author.

14. Since professional names (natori) require both talent and financial payments, the creation of the head (*iemoto*) of a new guild or branch has considerable economic as well as artistic implications. This system is such a part of the infrastructure of the Japanese arts that it has shown up even in the teaching of folk songs since the mid twentieth century.

15. The use of the noh flute may be why there are two flute players in the recording as shown in Figure 23.

16. In fact, he was wrong, for three singers and three shamisen are common in concert nagauta today, though *Hōrai* is frequently performed as a duet. One important contemporary factor is economic, since few musicians can afford to perform onstage in small numbers. In concerts as opposed to dance accompaniments, many persons must pay for the privilege of participating.

17. All the tempo markings in the transcriptions of this chapter indicate the tempo at the start of a passage and must not be considered to apply throughout the example.

18. *Hōrai* is found in the standard dance book, ed. Mori, *Nihon buyō kyoku shūran*, p. 122, but without references to any choreographers. The dance guild system operates like those of other traditional arts, so the wide variety of tempi that we see in the music may reflect differences of interpretation in various dance schools as well as differences in musical taste.

19. I recall a fascinating half hour observing a driver on the one-car Keifuku train in Kyoto. His turning of the speed handle and stepping on the brake pedal were as powerful as the stroke of a taiko kashira cadence pattern (see the Second View). They also were preluded by a proper vocal sound. Japanese labor movements in general are not made without such a "kakegoe," and may be equally filled with koshi.

20. The identification of the singers on recording III is based on the author's familiarity with their voices. Actually, we studied together under the same teachers in 1955–57.

21. The *matsu no ha* can be heard on the recording *Shamisen uta no oitachi to sono utsuri kawari* [Shamisen singing style and its change] (Columbia AL 5019–5022), record 2, item 14. The Eizō book misspells the name of the genre as *inda odori*.

22. *Shamisen uta no oitachi*, record 2, item 13.

23. As noted in the Interlude, shamisen accents are not necessarily those of a Western measure, so the word *offbeat* here may be a Western imposition.

24. Kiyomoto is one of the most lyrical of the narrative genres in kabuki. See Malm, *Japanese Music*, chaps. 8, 9.

SIXTH VIEW

1. One example is Earl Miner, *The Japanese Tradition in British and American Literature* (Princeton, N.J.: Princeton University Press, 1958).

2. See Signey Warschausky, "Yeats's Purgatory Plays," *Modern Drama* 7, no. 3 (December 1964): 278–86.

3. These comments originally appeared in the program notes for the first production of *Curlew River* and have been reprinted in the notes of the recording (London OSA A 4156), in Patricia Howard, *The Operas of Benjamin Britten* (New York: Praeger, 1969), pp. 182–83, and in David Herbert, ed., *The Operas of Benjamin Britten* (New York: Columbia University Press, 1979), at the start of the libretto. Comments on Britten's first noh experience are given in fine detail in the travel diary of Prince Ludwig of Hesse and the Rhine, published in Anthony Gishford, ed., *Tribute to Benjamin Britten* (London: Faber, 1963).

4. Other studies of the Britten opera are found in such works as Peter Evans, *The Music of Benjamin Britten* (Minneapolis: University of Minneapolis Press, 1979), pp. 467–80, Eric Walter White, *Benjamin Britten: His Life and Operas* (Berkeley and Los Angeles: University of California Press, 1970), pp. 205–13, and Gilbert L. Blout, "Britten's *Curlew River*, A Cultural Composite," *Literature East and West* 15, no. 1–2 (December 1971–June 1972): 632–45. Since this is a study in comparisons, I shall not refer to other scholars' opinions of *Curlew River* or its relation to noh. The impressions and opinions offered are mine only.

5. Noh masks are usually smaller than the actor's face. I have often thought that the constant visibility of the actor's chin movements has become part of the aesthetic of noh in the Zen sense of telling us that "this is not THIS."

6. Colin Graham, *Production Notes and Remarks on the Style of Performing "Curlew River"* (London: Faber & Faber, 1965), p. 3.

7. An English translation of Zeami's ideas on this subject is found in Izutsu and Izutsu, *Theory of Beauty* (see the Second View, n. 16, p. 203), pp. 97–104. The original texts of all of Zeami's writings are found in Nose Asaji, ed., *Zeami jurokubunshu hyōshaku* [An explanation of the sixteen works of Zeami] (Tokyo: Iwanami shoten, 1960).

8. Zeami, *Kadensho* (Tokyo: Sumiya-shinobe Institute, 1968), p. 48.

9. Izutsu and Izutsu, *Theory of Beauty*, pp. 128, 130. For the original text, see Minoru Nishio, ed., *Nihon koten bungaku taikei* (see the Third View, n. 4), vol. 65 (1965), p. 454.

10. Izutsu and Izutsu, *Theory of Beauty*, p. 133. Zeami attributes this saying to Mencius, but it seems to have actually come from the Chinese *Shu ching* [Book of history] of the second century B.C.

11. *Sumidagawa*, in *The Noh Drama*, ed. Japanese Classical Translation Committee (Tokyo: Tuttle, 1955), pp. 147–59.

12. The *Curlew River* libretto is found in the recording (London A 4156), the score (London: Faber & Faber, 1965), and the David Herbert edition of all of Britten's libretti (see n. 3 above). The Japanese sources used for this study were: Nogami Toyoichirō, ed., *Yōkyoku zenshū* (Tokyo: Chūō kōronsha, 1936), vol. 3, pp. 377–92; Yokomichi Mario and Omote Akira, eds., *Yōkyoku shū* (Tokyo: Iwanami shoten, 1960), vol. a, pp. 385–94; Koyama Hitoshi, ed., *Yōkyoku shū* (Tokyo: Kogakkan, 1973), vol. 1, pp. 502–16; Sanri Kentarō, ed., *Yōkyoku taikan* (Tokyo: Meiji shoin, 1954), vol. 4, pp. 1517–35; and Kanze Sesagon, ed., *Sumidagawa* (Tokyo: Hinoki shoten, 1952), *utaibon* [songbook] 27-4.

13. A memorial for the events is found in the Mokubo temple across the river from Asakusa. Apparently it was placed there after the drama made the story so famous rather than as a true historical record.

14. The jo ha kyū division is found in the 1936 *Yōkyoku zenshū* (see n. 12 above). The 1960 *Yōkyoku shū* merely uses eight numbered divisions, and the 1973 edition uses nine.

15. London A 4156.

16. The author is particularly grateful to Professor Kikkawa Eishi for arranging this important acquisition of nonpublic material. The Kanze production was broadcast on February 27, 1967. The cast was as follows: shite, Umewaka Rokuro; waki, Hōshō Yoichi; tsure, Hōshō Kan; kokata, Kakutō Naotaka; kōken, Umewaka Kisatoshi and Kakutō Ikuo; ji, Umewaka Yasuyuki, Umewaka Kagehide, Yamazaki Eitarō, Koyama Fumihiko, and others; hayashi, Tanaka Hitotsugu (flute), Seo Noritake (ō tsuzumi), and Uzama Toshi (ko tsuzumi). Since many people study noh singing, there are commercial recordings of *Sumidagawa* available that do not include the hayashi part. Two of them are King SKC 1027 (1967), for the Kanze school, and number 18 of Takenouchi Seiyū, ed., *Hōshō ryū hyakubanshū* (Tokyo: Chikuma shobō, 1960), for the Hōshō school. The latter includes traditional notation.

17. See *Sumidagawa* in note 12 above.

18. The translation is from Daniel Joseph Donahoe, *Early Christian Hymns* (London: T. Werner Laurie, n.d.), p. 41.

19. For example, in the traveller's prayer in the michiyuki and in the prayer for safety in the mondō before the katari section.

20. Note that the drums have not yet entered in the noh play.

21. In the NHK production, he does not wear a travelling hat as is seen in the utaibon drawing.

22. In the poetry collection *Gosenshū* (A.D. 951).

23. Foot stamps (*ashibyōshi*) are done only at specific places on a noh stage, large pots being placed beneath the stage at these points so that the proper tone quality will be produced.

24. The poem, by Lady Kunaikyō in the *Shin kokinshū* (ca. A.D. 1207), refers to a lover, not a child.

25. The field is located in Kyoto (Miyako), where the woman and child had lived.

26. Another use of the two patterns discussed here is seen in Example 26. Notation of the patterns for the ko tsuzumi is found in Figure 13 along with that of the ō tsuzumi mitsuji. To coordinate the examples from the two compositions studied in this chapter, notations of vocal parts from *Sumidagawa* conform to the Western convention of writing the tenor part in treble clef and the choral parts in bass. The specific pitch at which these parts are sung may vary in performance.

27. From this point on, examples from *Sumidagawa* will include direct translations under the romanization of the Japanese text to enhance one's appreciation of the relationship between the musical line and specific words. I wish to thank Professor Robert Brower of the Department of Far Eastern Languages and Literature at the University of Michigan for advice on the rendering of these words.

28. This alludes to a Confucian story involving the cries of a mother bird as the young birds leave.

29. Recall that the tomb is always present on the noh stage, but one does not "see" it until it is time to see it.

30. *Azuma* means the Tokyo (Edo) area, just as *Miyako* means Kyoto. The two terms have the same meaning as *East* and *West* in English.

31. This is a reference to a legend about a tree that one could see from a distance but disappeared when one got closer.

32. The sound heard in cassette example NN at the word *kage* (light) is not the striking of the gong but a stage accident that occurred as the waki prepared to bring the shite the Buddhist prayer gong.

33. This is a reference to the notion of Buddha as a moon that dispels ignorance and brings enlightenment.

34. The four-column excerpt from the noh songbook begins with this choral entrance. The child's entrance is partway down in the third column from the right.

35. Perhaps only those who have seen the melodramatic version of this play in the kabuki can appreciate how different but equally dramatic these two strikes on the gong can be in noh.

36. In the NHK videotape, the child moves to the waki corner diagonally across from the mother at the shite pillar. The utaibon drawing shows a different arrangement.

37. Donahoe, *Early Christian Hymns*, p. 213.

GLOSSARY
INDEX

Designer: Mark Ong
Compositor: G&S Typesetters, Inc.
Text: 11/13 Garamond
Display: Garamond
Printer: Malloy Lithographing, Inc.
Binder: John H. Dekker & Sons